DELEUZE AND THE PASSIONS

*Fig.* 1. Hieronymus Bosch, *Ship of Fools* (1490–1500)

First published in 2016 by punctum books, Earth, Milky Way. https://punctumbooks.com

ISBN-13: 978-0-9982375-4-1
ISBN-10: 0-9982375-4-X
Library of Congress Cataloging Data is available from the Library of Congress

Book design: Vincent W.J. van Gerven Oei
Cover image: Ghérasim Luca, *Passionnément* (1944). Private collection, Paris. © Micheline Catti-Ghérasim Luca.

This book has been made possible with a VENI grant from the Netherlands Organisation for Scientific Research (NWO).

# DELEUZE AND THE PASSIONS

EDITED BY
CECIEL MEIBORG &
SJOERD VAN TUINEN

Ⓟ

# Contents

# Introduction

*Ceciel Meiborg and Sjoerd van Tuinen*

> *paspas do passe passiopassion do*
> *ne do ne domi ne passi ne dominez pas*
> *ne dominez pas vos passions passives ne*
> *ne domino vos passio vos vos*
> *ssis vos passio ne dodo vos*
> *vos dominos d'or*
> *c'est domdommage do dodor*
> *do pas pas ne domi*
> *pas paspasse passio*
> — Ghérasim Luca, "Passionnément"[1]

In recent years the humanities, the social sciences, and neu-roscience have witnessed an "affective turn," especially in dis-courses around post-Fordist labor, the economic and ecological crisis, populism and identity politics, mental health, and politi-cal struggle.[2] This new awareness of affect remains unthinkable without the pioneering work of Gilles Deleuze, who, following Baruch Spinoza, displaced the traditional opposition of reason

1 Ghérasim Luca, "Passionnément," *Le chant de la carpe* (Paris: Le Soleil Noir, 1986), 87.
2 See for example Patricia Ticineto Clough and Jean Halley, eds., *The Affec-tive Turn: Theorizing the Social* (Durham: Duke University Press, 2007) and Melissa Gregg and Gregory J. Seigworth, ed., *The Affect Theory Reader* (Durham: Duke University Press, 2010).

and emotion with the new opposition between sad and joyful passions which diminish or increase our capacity to think and act. He thus replaced judgment with affect as the very movement of thought. While classical rationalism implies a moral judgment over and against emotions, the new one is an ethical evaluation of the rationality of emotions themselves. As Spinoza already put it: "we neither strive for, not will, neither want, nor desire anything because we judge it to be good; on the contrary, we judge something to be good because we strive for it, will it, want it, and desire it."[3]

For Spinoza, affect constitutes the bare activity of the world. An affect occurs when two finite modes of being (bodies or ideas), each defined by its *conatus* or its striving for persistence, encounter each other, leading to either an increase or a decrease of their respective powers to affect and to be affected. Affects, then, are collective becomings, i.e., processes or passages of desire individuated by the manner in which beings seek to augment their power to engage with others. They are primordial to, albeit inseparable from, sensations, emotions, feelings, tastes, perceptions, beliefs, meanings, and all other forms of cognition. Whereas the more articulated and exchangeable forms of feeling and cognizing are already individuated and personalized "affections," affects cannot be reduced to the different ways in which they are embodied and the intellectual states in which they are interpreted. Rather, they contain a transformative potential. For Deleuze, affective becomings make up the ontological element of a transcendental empiricism, a differential element of forces (Friedrich Nietzsche) or tendencies (Henri Bergson) that is autonomous, neutral and eternal. Thought, or the problem of how to orient ourselves within this element, is a matter of empirically and experientially learning to compose with affects.

Spinoza distinguishes passive affects that are prompted by an exterior force, and active affects that stem from an internal cause. Ideas or bodies are active when their actions follow only

3  Baruch Spinoza, *Ethics,* trans. Edwin Curley (London: Penguin Classics, 1996), III P9.S.

from themselves, whereas they are passive to the extent that they depend on other bodies and ideas. Passion, as Spinoza puts it, is "a part of Nature which cannot be perceived clearly and distinctly through itself."[4] Because of its finitude, however, no mode is purely active. All activity is embedded in the lived world along the lines of passions. Whereas the Cartesian "clear and distinct" offers an image of autonomous thought ("I think") as immediately self-transparent consciousness of self-evident (true) ideas, in reality thought — the active-passive becoming of ideas — is never separable from the obscure and the confused, in other words, the "unconscious." This is why Deleuze redistributes the rationalist economy of light, even if he does so in a way more indebted to the Leibnizian theory of the unconscious than Spinoza: whereas active affects are distinct but obscure, passions are clear but confused.[5] Adequate ideas distinctly express their immanent causality (pure immanence), but as actions or events their visibility amounts only to little glimmerings in the night. Consciousness or clear perception, by contrast, is of the order of effects; it is composed of passions (impure immanence) that express the powers of others and ourselves confusedly.

The trajectory of liberation that defines Spinoza's *Ethics* is the movement of learning by which thought, born in bondage and confusion, passes into the adequate comprehension of affect and acquires its full potential (the state of beatitude). In practice, then, thought always begins with the passions. These are the beliefs, perceptions, representations, and opinions that attach us to the world and that, by giving us an initial orientation, force and enable us to think. From language to consciousness, everything finds its basis in passion, which makes up the very material of which our lives and thoughts are composed. As soon as we are confronted with empirical knowledge and human affairs, no matter whether this concerns emotions in psychology and sociology, sensation in art, passion in theology, or the struggle

4   Ibid., III P3.S.
5   Gilles Deleuze, *Difference and Repetition,* trans. Paul Patton (New York: Columbia University Press, 1994), 196–98, 208–14.

with opinion in philosophy, we are always dealing with passive affects. Rather than being a philosophy *of* passions, we should therefore say that Deleuze's philosophy puts passion at the core of thought. It is through passion that we acquire our power of action and thus a power to produce concepts or what Spinoza calls common notions, which are adequate expressions of our communal being. The philosophical task for Deleuze is not one of banning the passions from thought, but rather a question of "How do we extend the passions, give them an extension that they do not have of themselves?"[6] To become free is to socialize the passions in a political body. "The people must be individualized, not according to the persons within it, but according to the affects it experiences simultaneously or successively."[7]

The liberation of thought is a becoming active of passion, which always involves joy, since "there is a necessary joy in creation."[8] Joyful passions bring us closer to our volition, while sad passions, on the contrary, weaken our power, binding desire to the illusions of consciousness and separating us from our power to act. Put differently, joyful passions augment our power, while sad passions enslave us. Instead of truth as ultimate criterion of judgment, the only principle according to which affective becomings can be selected and evaluated is the extent to which they proliferate joy. "A mode of existence is good or bad, noble or vulgar, complete or empty, independently of Good and Evil or any transcendent value: there are never any criteria other than the tenor of existence, the intensification of life."[9] If it takes a lot of inventiveness or imagination to become able to diagnose our present becomings, however, this is because be-

---

6   Gilles Deleuze, *Desert Islands and Other Texts: 1953–1974,* ed. David Lapoujade, trans. Michael Taormina (Los Angeles/New York: Semiotext(e), 2004), 167.

7   Gilles Deleuze and Félix Guattari, *A Thousand Plateaus: Capitalism and Schizophrenia,* trans. Brian Massumi (Minneapolis: University of Minnesota Press, 1987), 341.

8   Deleuze, *Desert Islands,* 134.

9   Gilles Deleuze and Félix Guattari, *What Is Philosophy?,* trans. Hugh Tomlinson and Graham Burchell (New York: Columbia University Press, 1994), 74.

comings are always composite. Desire is a heterogeneously determined mixture, like a line of experimentation traversing a
plane on which becomings find their consistency: "there is no
desire but assembling, assembled, desire."[10] Upholding the empiricist principle of the externality of relations, Deleuze claims
that within an assemblage "the relations themselves are assigned
a sense, a direction, an irreversibility, and an exclusivity according to the passions."[11] Thus in an assemblage there are always
paradoxical factors at work. Health, as Nietzsche has shown,
is not so much the absence of sickness, but rather a composition of contrasting tendencies that leads toward less sickness
and more health.[12] Likewise, Deleuze discovers in Primo Levi
or Yasser Arafat — but also in philosophy itself — a kind of glory
that only occurs in relation to the shame that constitutes their
initial motivation.[13] In each case, the relation between the terms
(health/sickness, glory/shame) is never a simple opposition, as
if their difference was already analytically included in them. Instead, this difference depends on a whole constellation of exterior forces, on "the dominant affective tonality" which recruits
desire to increase its power.[14]

Spinoza shows how the recruitment of desire traditionally
takes place through the tyrants and priests who inspire sad passions in us, just as Karl Marx demonstrates how in capitalism
enslavement primarily takes place through employment relations. As Frédéric Lordon has pointed out, Fordism, marking
capitalism's earlier stages, is based on a passionate servitude
that instigates and feeds off the fear of starvation when one

10  Deleuze and Guattari, *A Thousand Plateaus*, 399.
11  Deleuze, *Desert Islands*, 166.
12  Friedrich Nietzsche, *Ecce Homo*, ed. and trans. Walter Kaufmann, pub-
    lished together with *On the Genealogy of Morals*, ed. Walter Kaufmann,
    trans. Walter Kaufmann and Reginald J. Hollingdale (New York: Vintage
    Books, 1989), 222–3.
13  Deleuze and Guattari, *What Is Philosophy?*, 107, and Gilles Deleuze, "The
    Grandeur of Yasser Arafat," trans. Timothy S. Murhpy, *Discourse* 20, no. 3
    (1998): 30–33.
14  Frédéric Lordon, *Willing Slaves of Capital: Spinoza & Marx on Desire*,
    trans. Gabriel Ash (London/ New York: Verso Books, 2014), 24.

would quit working in the assembly line.[15] Similarly, the work of Deleuze and Guattari on capitalism and schizophrenia can be read as an encyclopedia of the passions that constitute the affective infrastructure of the *socius* of contemporary capitalism. These include sad passions such as shame, spite, guilt, stupidity, mistrust, weariness, fatigue, fatalism, cynicism, ignorance, hope, anguish, disgust, contempt, cowardice, hatred, laziness, avidity, regret, despair, mockery, malversation, and self-abasement. Whereas the deterritorializing forces of capital constantly demand from us a "passional betrayal" of the dominant social structure, these same passions need to be controlled on the level of our private lives (i.e., the Oedipal triangle). This is why in the formation of a well-emancipated individual the priestly origins of western subjectivity can still be clearly discerned. The contemporary culture of health and abstinence, as Slavoj Žižek has famously pointed out, is a culture of safe sex, smoking bans, coffee without caffeine, intolerance for misogynic jokes, wars without casualties, and so forth.[16] But capitalism could not exist if it did not also inspire joy, love, courage, and perhaps even beatitude. Fordism already compensated for fear by installing a hope for more consumption. Today we witness "the spectacle of the happily dominated" of the managerial class, the flex worker, the citizen-consumer, the bean-roasting hipster, the *homo economicus,* and the self-managed team.[17] It is only in late capitalism that individuation takes place primarily in the form of the self-centered subject that is working for his or her self-realization. With the rise of the self-entrepreneur we can perhaps speak for the first time, despite the manifest oxymoron, of a veritable voluntary servitude, in which enslavement is immediately fulfilled by joyful passions.

Philosophy, the passion of doing philosophy, is far from innocent in this respect. It represses the creative act of thinking by

15  Lordon, *Willing Slaves of Capital,* 23–28.
16  Slavoj Žižek, *Demanding the Impossible,* ed. Yong-june Park (Cambridge: Polity Press, 2013), 83–85.
17  Ibid., xi–xii.

enslaving thought to that haggard image of self-sufficient and self-gratifying rationality that it inevitably produces of itself. As Deleuze and Guattari ask us: "Is there anything more passional than pure reason? Is there a colder, more extreme, more self-interested passion than the Cogito?"[18] This explains why Deleuze hardly lives up to the caricature of the affirmative thinker of spontaneous happiness that still dominates his legacy.[19] There is joy in destruction, especially in the destruction of Reason. Spinoza already pointed at the common disregard for passions of the thinkers of his era, claiming that "they attribute the cause of human impotence and inconstancy, not to the common power of Nature, but to I know not what vice of human nature, which they therefore bewail, or laugh at, or disdain, or (as usually happens) curse."[20] Working along the naturalist axis of Lucretius-Spinoza-Nietzsche and extending it into a Humean "empiricist conversion," Deleuze equally maintains that the inseparability of reason and passion is in no sense anti-intellectualist or irrationalist. Rather, their inseparability is critical, since it protects reason from its self-imposed stupidity (*bêtise*) by relating it to the unthought, i.e. the distinct but obscure forces that condition it. And it is clinical, since for the naturalist, it is here that thought becomes possessed by a "power of aggression and selection."[21] A thought only reaches consistency and prominence in "isolated and passionate cries" that deny what everybody knows and what nobody can deny. At the beginning of thought, we discover not a transparent self, but a self dissolved in the interstices of its passions, a veritably schizophrenic thought-drama: "There is always another breath in my breath, another thought in my thought, another possession in what I possess, a thousand

---

18  Deleuze and Guattari, *A Thousand Plateaus*, 130.

19  "Reading Deleuze is like a Bacardi Rum advertisement. It is an advertisement without body: one never sees Bacardi rum; one only sees that everybody is happy" (Boris Groys, seminar "Immaterial Communication," in *Concepts on the Move*, eds. Annette W. Balkema and Henk Slager, 50–67 [Amsterdam/New York: Rodopi, 2002], 65).

20  Spinoza, *Ethics*, III Preface.

21  Deleuze, *Difference and Repetition*, xx.

things and a thousand beings implicated in my complications: every true thought is an aggression."[22]

Sharing Hegel's question of how thought finds its way into the world and vice versa, Deleuze discerns an answer in Antonin Artaud and his concept of the theater of cruelty. The destruction of the established image of thought involves a laborious ploughing through thick layers of passion. Only on the brink of exhaustion, where thought risks to be entirely submerged, do bursts and leaps appear that uncover a glimpse of spontaneous, non-prefigured, and non-subjugated thought-desire. Every true philosophical concept comes into being as a passionate cry. The philosopher faces a schizophrenic task, which "is less a question of recovering meaning than of destroying the word, of conjuring up the affect, and of transforming the painful passion of the body into a triumphant action, obedience into command [...]."[23] This is where philosophy and literature meet, in defamiliarizing the familiar, not by taking a "philosophical distance" from the world, but by the full immersion of thought in the world and its material, i.e., passional reality. Ghérasim Luca's "Passionnément," for that matter, is not so much an act carried out on the mere surface of language, but rather an engagement with the limits of language. By stretching and condensing, by having it bear the weight of what it is not, language abandons its lofty Olympian throne of dialectical reason judging over the world in clear and distinct propositions, and affirms both itself and the world in the production of a new intensity. Or in the words of Deleuze: "The entire language spins and varies in order to disengage a final block of sound, a single breath at the limit of the cry, JE T'AIME PASSIONNÉMENT ("I love you passionately")."[24]

---

22  Gilles Deleuze, *The Logic of Sense,* trans. Mark Lester (New York: Columbia University Press, 1990), 298.

23  Ibid., 88.

24  Gilles Deleuze, *Essays Critical and Clinical,* trans. Daniel W. Smith and Michael A. Greco (Minneapolis: University of Minnesota Press, 1997), 110.

*The contributions*

It is well-known that Deleuze finds in Hegel the ultimate betrayal of this naturalist practice of philosophy. With thinkers such as Jean Wahl, Jean-Paul Sartre, Alexandre Kojève, and Jean Hyppolite, the philosophical landscape of his formative years was dominated by Hegelianism. But as Moritz Gansen points out in his contribution, the unhappy consciousness that drives Hegel's philosophical system is a thorn in the flesh of philosophy. Following Nietzsche, Deleuze considers the unhappy consciousness "only the Hegelian version of the bad conscience," that internalized guilt and restlessness which multiplies and glorifies sad passions. The endeavor of escaping the totalizing tendencies of the Hegelian dialectics has defined his entire oeuvre.

In his philosophical pursuit of joy and creativity, Deleuze seeks to circumvent the dialectical pursuit of reason, which "represents our slavery and our subjection as something superior which makes us reasonable beings."[25] Samantha Bankston demonstrates how a shift from a philosophy of judgment to a philosophy of affect implies a more radical shift from Being to becoming than the movement of the Hegelian concept allows for. Traditionally, reason forces upon thought the categories of Being, which are analogy, identity, opposition, resemblance. To accommodate for the transformative potential of a philosophy of affect, Deleuze develops a new, twofold concept of becoming. Sensory becoming refers to the immanent logic that makes up the composite nature of assemblages. Absolute becoming amounts to the becoming active, a "counter-effectuation" of the image of thought.

Adopting the Nietzschean project of inverting Platonism and tracing the dialectic to its Socratic roots, Deleuze returns to the Greek dramatic setting of the agon with its rivalry between the claimants of truth. The first time he systematically takes up the theme of distinguishing "the true pretender from the false

25  Gilles Deleuze, *Nietzsche and Philosophy,* trans. Hugh Tomlinson (New York: Columbia University Press, 1983), 92–93.

one,"[26] is in the treatment of jealousy in *Proust and Signs*. As Arjen Kleinherenbrink demonstrates, the jealous lover can only distinguish himself from the other claimants and rightfully claim his beloved one if he reaches her true essence. The passion of jealousy enables him to become active, to make a difference. It does not, however, lead him to her true essence, but rather to the truth that her essence will keep on escaping him. Or, as Deleuze later puts it: "[D]oes not this passionate search for true opinion lead the Platonists to an aporia," the gray zone in which truth and falsity become indiscernible?[27]

Sjoerd van Tuinen further develops Deleuze's method of dramatization by staging the priest and the philosopher as the two competing claimants to the concept of *ressentiment*. They embody respectively a nihilistic sense of the concept of *ressentiment* and a speculative sense. The priest moralistically judges others because of their *ressentiment*, while the philosopher immanently affirms *ressentiment,* rather than opposing it. Historically speaking, this difference leads to a parting of the ways in the discourse on *ressentiment* after Nietzsche. By psychologizing *ressentiment* and fixating it as the secretive emotion of guilty individuals, authors such as Max Scheler and René Girard have instrumentalized the concept of *ressentiment* to turn it against the voices of minorities. Deleuze, by contrast, is a genealogist who affirms *ressentiment* as an inherently political passion open to a drama of divergent becomings. Ultimately, the difference between the priest and the philosopher is not a question of truth, but of passion. As conceptual personae, they are two passions of thought and thus two different powers of imagination and becoming. Whereas the priest judges on the basis of empirical *facts,* only the philosopher — Nietzsche's philosopher-legislator — possesses the transcendental *right* to wield the concept of *ressentiment*.

Likewise, Jason Read points out that a philosophy of affect always carries the risk of interiorization, in which the intimate

---

26  Deleuze, *Logic of Sense,* 254.
27  Ibid., 148.

takes precedence over the social and the social is reduced to a set of individuals. Combining Spinoza's inherently political account of affect with Gilbert Simondon's theory of individuation, Deleuze and Guattari in the *Capitalism and Schizophrenia* series put forward two different ways in which this risk can be avoided. *Anti-Oedipus* provides a history of the dominant affects that determine the structure of feeling, while focusing on resisting reductive accounts of the social, with Sigmund Freud as its polemical target. *A Thousand Plateaus,* on the other hand, reaches beyond the historical determinations of affect by tracing the affects of capitalism that pass between the dominant passions, indicating possible lines of flight.

Following Deleuze and Guattari, Benoît Dillet argues that ideology critique is ineffective since it merely critiques a system of beliefs, rather than diagnosing the passions that are at the basis of capitalism. The strict separation of psycho-social passions and economic interests in ideology critique reinforces a mechanism of neutralization of the joyful passions, because it denies the desire that is at the very core of capitalism. Instead, Deleuze and Guattari propose to expand the project of ideology critique to the project of noology critique, which refers to the study of the images of thought and their historicity. This means that the materiality and the passionate infrastructure that preconditions the dogmatic image of thought is taken into account.

Louis-Georges Schwartz points out that the image regimes as presented by Deleuze in his books on cinema emerge dialectically from the labor-capital relations (formal versus real subsumption of labor under capital). With the full subsumption of labor — when labor itself and being available for labor become indiscernible — the image regime of the twenty-first century is what Schwartz calls Cinema Hostis. This regime pivots upon an antagonism; characters become each other's enemies and the camera is the enemy of all. Just as each of Deleuze's two image regimes expresses affects in its own signs and forms, with Cinema Hostis affects become weaponized molar ready-mades and lose their transhuman and deterritorializing character, immobilizing their creative potential.

David Liu takes up the theme of the possibility of escape in asking us: When Deleuze jumped out of the window, toward his death — just as Luca jumped into the Seine one year earlier — did he deframe or reframe the passions? Should we consider Deleuze's suicide a line of flight or a line of death, or both at the same time?[28] The Spinozist division between joyful and sad passions forces a binary logic upon thought, which denies the fundamentally paradoxical and heterogenous nature of becoming. This dichotomy is only intensified in capitalism, in which you are either productive or unproductive, happy or sad. Deleuze may have escaped this capitalist dualism with his public suicide, which enabled him to affect and be affected at once. While implying his irrevocable death, his suicide also forces us to think about how life always carries death within it.

With Liu we see how even Deleuze's death impassions our thinking. To return to Deleuze's question "How do we extend the passions?" we can maintain that he has indicated many openings for doing so. With this volume we aim to provide a systematic study of Deleuze's taxonomy of the passions and their importance for a thinking that reaches beyond itself, whether this is effectuated by tracing the sad passions that Deleuze tries to escape (Gansen, Bankston) or by engaging with strategies that integrate sad passions with joyful passions (Kleinherenbrink, Van Tuinen), by diagnosing the passions that make up the affective infrastructure of capitalism (Dillet, Read, Schwartz) or by questioning the dichotomy of the joyful and sad passions altogether (Liu). We hope that, between the lines, you will read the passion that made us compose this volume, that this book will move you, and equip you with tools to extend this movement.

---

28  Cf. "This, precisely, is the fourth danger: the line of flight crossing the wall, getting out of the black holes, but instead of connecting with other lines and each time augmenting its valence, *turning to destruction, abolition pure and simple the passion of abolition.* Like Kleist's line of flight, and the strange war he wages; like suicide, double suicide, a way out that turns the line of flight into a line of death" (Deleuze and Guattari, *A Thousand Plateaus,* 227).

# 1

# "Everywhere There Are Sad Passions": Gilles Deleuze and the Unhappy Consciousness

*Moritz Gansen*

> *Hegel… Hegel? Quoi, qu'est-ce que c'est ça?*
> — Gilles Deleuze[1]

## Philosophical sensibility

From the very beginning of his philosophical career, Gilles Deleuze defined philosophy as the "creation of concepts."[2] Such creation, however, was never a matter of "pure" philosophy, "'pure' theory," at least if philosophy and theory were to be understood in a "traditional," in a reflexive and rationalist sense, in

---

1 Gilles Deleuze, "Spinoza: Session 4," lecture, Université Paris-VIII, Paris, France, January 6, 1981, http://www2.univ-paris8.fr/deleuze/article. php3?id_article=9, accessed September 28, 2016.
2 While this definition is most famously presented in *What Is Philosophy?* (Gilles Deleuze and Félix Guattari, *What Is Philosophy?*, trans. Hugh Tomlinson and Graham Burchell [New York: Columbia University Press, 1994], passim), Deleuze used it from very early on. In 1956, for instance, he opened an essay on Bergson with the assertion that "[a] great philosopher creates new concepts" (Gilles Deleuze, *Desert Islands and Other Texts: 1953–1974,* ed. David Lapoujade, trans. Michael Taormina [Los Angeles: Semiotext(e), 2004], 22).

the sense of a "dogmatic image of thought."[3] Instead, the philosophical creation of concepts was always mediated by certain affects, by passions, passing through the non-philosophical. Accordingly, what Deleuze said about the late Michel Foucault was equally true of himself: "Thinking was never a matter of theory. It was to do with problems of life. It was life itself."[4]

This vital conception of thinking, one might say, constitutes Deleuze's very own image of thought, and it conditions his "philosophical sensibility."[5] After all, at least in hindsight, his interest in specific philosophers seems to be guided by an implicit system of affects, organized around the main coordinates of "joy" on the one hand and "sadness" on the other. For Deleuze, philosophy, considered as a matter of life, had to be "joyful." As he told Jeanette Colombel in an interview in 1969, the true power of philosophy, even where it is critical and destructive, "springs from affirmation, from joy, from a cult of affirmation and joy, from the exigency of life against those who would mutilate and mortify it."[6] Consequently, his writings on the history of philosophy focused on authors whom he considered a challenge to a philosophical tradition marked by rationalism on the one hand and negativity on the other. Among them were Lucretius, David Hume, and Henri Bergson, but "all tended," as he explained, "toward the great Spinoza-Nietzsche identity."[7]

This attention for a supposed countercurrent in the history of philosophy,[8] championing an affirmative and vital understanding of philosophy, was paired with a determined rejection of

3    On the "image of thought," cf. Gilles Deleuze, *Difference and Repetition,* trans. Paul Patton (New York: Columbia University Press, 1994), 129–67.
4    Gilles Deleuze, *Negotiations 1972–1990,* trans. Martin Joughin (New York: Columbia University Press), 105, trans. modified.
5    Deleuze, "Spinoza: Session 4."
6    Deleuze, *Desert Islands,* 144.
7    Deleuze, *Negotiations,* 135, trans. modified; cf. ibid., 5–7.
8    Despite his appeals to a clandestine counter-lineage, one should not forget that Deleuze, as Giuseppe Bianco points out, "essentially wrote about the authors whom his professors had taught." Among these professors were, most notably, Ferdinand Alquié, Georges Canguilhem, Maurice de Gandillac, Jean Hyppolite and Jean Wahl (François Dosse, *Gilles Deleuze,*

philosophy in its present state, evidently governed by a taste for negativity. For Deleuze, as for many others, this taste for negativity was paradigmatically embodied in the prevalence of a particular French Hegelianism, which, under the name of Georg Wilhelm Friedrich Hegel himself, became the target of an often relentless critique, a critique that to some may have seemed excessive. As for instance Jean Wahl remarked in his generally favorable review of *Nietzsche and Philosophy,* one could get the impression that there was, "in the author, a sort of *ressentiment* toward Hegelian philosophy, which sometimes dictates him passages of great rigor, but sometimes also risks to deceive him."[9] And indeed, in his letter to Michel Cressole, Deleuze admitted that his persistent anti-Hegelianism was doubtlessly a matter of affects: "What I most detested," he explained, "was Hegelianism and dialectics."[10]

However, given that affects are inevitably intertwined with philosophy as a matter of life, Deleuze's passionate plea against Hegelianism is more than an idiosyncratic expression of personal preference. It needs to be understood in terms of a systematic philosophical "symptomatology" and "typology."[11] Approaching Deleuze's critique precisely from the standpoint of such an affective symptomatology, the present essay offers a — by no means exhaustive — reconstruction of an important aspect of the historical and systematic conditions of Deleuze's anti-Hegelianism, arguing that his rejection of Hegel on the grounds of a theory of affects draws upon a particular figure of an inherently "sad" mode of thinking, the "unhappy consciousness," which was introduced into French philosophy by Deleuze's teacher Jean Wahl. It is precisely against the backdrop of a Hegelianism con-

*and Félix Guattari: Intersecting Lives,* trans. Deborah Glassman [New York: Columbia University Press, 2010], 109–10).

9   Jean Wahl, "Nietzsche et la philosophie," *Revue de Métaphysique et de Morale* 68.3 (1963): 352–79, at 353. Unless indicated otherwise, all translations of passages cited from French editions are mine.

10  Deleuze, *Negotiations,* 6.

11  Gilles Deleuze, *Nietzsche and Philosophy,* trans. Hugh Tomlinson (New York: Columbia University Press, 2006), 75.

sidered as an "enterprise of ressentiment and the unhappy consciousness" that Deleuze seeks to develop and highlight, with the help of his readings of Baruch Spinoza and Friedrich Nietzsche, his own affirmative conception of philosophy.[12]

### A Hegelian horizon

In 1968, in his preface to *Difference and Repetition,* Deleuze suggested that his book should be read in light of a current of "generalized anti-Hegelianism," a valorization of difference and repetition over identity, negativity, and dialectics, which, according to him, was indicated in Martin Heidegger, in structuralism, in the contemporary novel, and so on.[13] At the time, however, Hegel had only recently been fully naturalized within French academic philosophy. In 1967, for example, Jean Hyppolite, arguably the most important French Hegel scholar of his generation,[14] was planning to establish a "Center for Hegelian Studies" at the Collège de France (a plan thwarted by his death a year later), and in 1968 Hegel appeared on the syllabus for the written *agrégation* for the first time.[15] After a long process of rehabilitation, even revaluation, Hegel had become ubiquitous, and, as Deleuze's colleague and friend François Châtelet asserted, he had been found to determine

> a horizon, a language, a code, within which we still are today [sc. in 1968]. Hegel, by this fact, is our Plato: the one who

12  Deleuze, *Desert Islands,* 144, translation modified.
13  Deleuze, *Difference and Repetition,* xix.
14  Most notably, Hyppolite accomplished the first French translation of Hegel's *Phenomenology of Spirit* in 1939 and prepared an extensive commentary, published in 1946, *Genesis and Structure of Hegel's Phenomenology of Spirit,* trans. Samuel Cherniak and John Heckman (Evanston: Northwestern University Press, 1974).
15  Cf. Alan Schrift, "The Effects of the Agrégation de Philosophie on Twentieth-Century French Philosophy," *Journal of the History of Philosophy* 46.3 (2008): 449–73, at 458.

delimits — ideologically or scientifically, positively or nega-
tively — the theoretical possibilities of theory.[16]

There was hence an entire generation of young French intellectuals who were formed within these (neo-)Hegelian limits, and
many of them seemed compelled to question, in one way or another, the authority of the alleged master thinker and his latest
disciples. As Foucault noted in his homage to Hyppolite — his
teacher at the Lycée Henri-IV and predecessor at the Collège de
France — there was an "entire epoch, whether in logic or epis-
temology, whether in Marx or Nietzsche, [...] trying to escape
from Hegel," never quite sure whether he was not already waiting for them, behind another dialectical ruse, "immobile and
elsewhere."[17]

Perhaps Foucault wrote these lines with Deleuze in mind.
The latter had also been Hyppolite's student in the 1940s, both
at the Lycée Henri-IV and at the Sorbonne, and he was (and he
had been for quite some time) indubitably trying to escape from
Hegel, indeed, among others, through Nietzsche. As a student,
Deleuze had inevitably been exposed to Hegelian thinking, to
the "Hegelian triads" that Hyppolite, as he recalled, "pounded
out [...] with his fist."[18] Therefore, one can assume that he "knew
his Hegel," despite the fact that he did not "admire" him and his
thinking, and hence had "no reason to write about [him]."[19] In

16  François Châtelet, *Hegel* (Paris: Editions du Seuil, 1968), 13.
17  Michel Foucault, "The Order of Discourse," trans. Ian McLeod, in *Untying
    the Text: A Post-Structuralist Reader,* ed. Robert Young, 51–77 (London:
    Routledge, 1981), 74.
18  Gilles Deleuze, quoted in Giuseppe Bianco, "Jean Hyppolite et Ferdinand
    Alquié," in *Aux sources de la pensée de Gilles Deleuze,* ed. Stéphan Leclerc,
    91–101 (Paris: Vrin/Sils Maria, 2006), 92n2; translated in Dosse, *Gilles
    Deleuze and Félix Guattari,* 95. Alain Badiou has remarked that "there was
    within him [Hyppolite] a subterranean negativity, a primordial 'no' about
    which we knew little but which was constantly at work" (Alain Badiou,
    *Pocket Pantheon: Figures of Postwar Philosophy,* trans. David Macey [Lon-
    don: Verso, 2009], 53).
19  Deleuze, *Desert Islands,* 144.

this sense, to be more precise, Deleuze's attitude is perhaps best rendered in a short passage he wrote about Nietzsche:

> It has been said that Nietzsche did not know his Hegel. In the sense that one does not know one's opponent well. On the other hand we believe that the Hegelian movement, the different Hegelian factions were familiar to him.[20]

The Hegelian movement familiar to Deleuze was, as mentioned before, a very particular one. As Foucault summarized much later, when looking back upon the years of his philosophical formation in a long interview with Duccio Trombadori, the prevailing French Hegelianism around the middle of the twentieth century was "permeated with phenomenology and existentialism, centered on the theme of the unhappy consciousness."[21] Precisely this is the context of Deleuze's "affective" critique of Hegel.

*The unhappy consciousness*

The notion of the "unhappy consciousness" became prominent in France in the wake of the reintroduction of Hegel into French philosophy in the mid and late 1920s. After Hegel had for a long time, and especially in the context of the Franco-Prussian War and its aftermath, been considered the architect of a deadening and totalizing, a panlogicist and even Pan-Germanist system,[22]

---

20 Deleuze, *Nietzsche and Philosophy*, 8.
21 Michel Foucault, "Interview with Michel Foucault," trans. Robert Hurley, in *The Essential Works of Michel Foucault, 1954–1984: Power,* ed. James D. Faubion, 239–97 (New York: The New Press, 2000), 246.
22 For a particularly striking example, cf. Henri Bergson, "Discours en séance publique de l'académie des sciences morales et politiques," in Henri Bergson, *Mélanges,* ed. André Robinet (Paris: Presses Universitaire de France, 1972), 1113, where Bergson links a Hegelian taste to the German invasion of Belgium in 1914, declaring that contemporary German philosophy was "simply the intellectual transposition of its [Germany's] brutality, of its appetites, and of its vices. […] Germany, having definitely become a predatory nation, refers itself to Hegel, like a Germany taken by moral beauty

he was now being rediscovered following the publication of the so-called *Early Theological Writings* (*Theologische Jugendschriften*) in 1907. Philosophers like Wahl and Alexandre Koyré suddenly began to see a different Hegel, one who seemed to exhibit very little of what previous readers had so fiercely criticized.[23] Read in productive conjunction for instance with the works of Søren Kierkegaard and Heidegger, these theological writings were reconnected to the *Phenomenology of Spirit* and interpreted in terms of a philosophy of concrete subjective experience, a philosophy, in other words, of existence. Before and beneath the systematic endeavors of the later years, Wahl and Koyré found a "human, vibrant, suffering Hegel."[24] "Behind the philosopher," they discovered, as Wahl put it, "the theologian, and behind the rationalist the romantic."[25] The young Hegel, it seemed, had actually anticipated the existential critique of his older self,[26] he had "in some measure," as Hyppolite would claim, "foreseen Kierkegaard."[27]

Within this new reading, the unhappy consciousness came to be assigned an absolutely central role, most extensively developed in Wahl's *Le malheur de la conscience dans la philosophie de Hegel*. If the *Phenomenology of Spirit* formed a propaedeutic to the system, the unhappy consciousness, already conceptually present in the early theological writings, embodied a kind of

would declare itself faithful to Kant or as a sentimental Germany would invoke Jacobi or Schopenhauer."

23 Cf. especially Jean Wahl, *Le malheur de la conscience dans la philosophie de Hegel*, 2nd ed. (Paris: Presses Universitaire de France, 1951); Alexandre Koyré, "Hegel à Iéna" and "Note sur la langue et la terminologie hégéliennes," in *Études d'histoire de la pensée philosophique* (Paris: Gallimard, 1961), 135–204; moreover Jean Hyppolite, "Les travaux de jeunesse de Hegel d'après des ouvrages récents," *Revue de Métaphysique et de Morale* 42.3 (1935): 399–426 and 42.4: 549–78; Jean Hyppolite, "Vie et prise de conscience de la vie dans la philosophie hégélienne d'Iéna," *Revue de Métaphysique et de Morale* 45.1 (1938): 45–61.

24 Koyré, "Hegel à Iéna," 137.

25 Wahl, *Le malheur de la conscience dans la philosophie de Hegel*, v.

26 Ibid., vii.

27 Jean Hyppolite, "Discours d'introduction," *Hegel-Studien*, Beiheft 3 (1966): 11–13, at 11.

atavism within it, an expression of an "existential *vibrato*"[28] that, according to Wahl, subtended Hegel's philosophy as a whole. In order to have become philosophically graspable, or conceivable, the unhappy consciousness must have had its specific truth in an actual crisis in Hegel's own concrete subjective (i.e., biographical) experience: the experience of an unattainable remainder that, although the object of the most profound desire, must forever, and constitutively, remain out of reach. Where Hegel's project grows into a striving for the creation of a philosophical system, it is at its core, for Wahl, "an effort toward the rationalization of a ground [*fond*] that reason does not attain,"[29] a sublimation, in other words, of an absolutely insuperable tension. And since the experience of an absolute unattainability, as an experience that leaves the subject grounded in nothing but its own despair, is here also a fundamentally religious experience,[30] Hegel is easily approximated to Kierkegaard, the "true" philosopher of the unhappy consciousness, who is himself, "against the system," "an unhappy consciousness."[31] Hegel's notion of the un-

---

28  Châtelet, *Hegel*, 11.

29  Wahl, *Le malheur de la conscience dans la philosophie de Hegel*, 108.

30  Wahl and Hyppolite have pointed out that the unhappy consciousness, besides being a determinate moment in the *Phenomenology of Spirit*, can also be read as an adaptation of Hegel's earlier theological writings. Although he does not explicate this in the *Phenomenology*, it can be said that the dialectic of the unhappy consciousness presents a phenomenology of religious experience in three historical stages. Its first stage, then, is the positing of an infinite immutable essence beyond the reach of a changing, inessential consciousness: Judaism, or the "reign of the Father." Its second moment is the realization of the contradiction, the immediate incarnation of the immutable, which, in its immediacy, remains just as unattainable: Christ, or the "reign of the Son." In its third moment, finally, the unhappy consciousness develops "to the point of complete self-negation," toward "actual sacrifice," in order to overcome its unhappiness: the Church, or the "reign of Spirit" (Hyppolite, *Genesis and Structure of Hegel's Phenomenology of Spirit*, 190–215; cf. also Wahl, *Le malheur de la conscience dans la philosophie de Hegel*, 10–118).

31  Jean Wahl, *Études kierkegaardiennes* (Paris: Aubier, 1938), 112. According to Wahl, there is, in the young Hegel and in Kierkegaard, "the same revolt against concepts, the same affirmation of subjective feeling on the one hand and being on the other, insofar as both are irreducible to concepts,

happy consciousness is understood as prefiguring the Kierkeg-aardian notion of existential despair:[32] "As long as consciousness does nothing but produce a beyond that it endeavors to attain in vain, spirit cannot find its peace."[33] It is in this existential experi-ence, then, according to Wahl, that we discover the root of the dialectic in a consciousness of internal tension and contradic-tion.

In Hegel's *Phenomenology,* the narrative of the process of the appearance of spirit, the unhappy consciousness follows upon the stoic and the skeptic consciousness in the problematic de-velopment of the freedom of self-consciousness, which in turn follows upon the more famous formation of self-consciousness in the dialectic of lord and bondsman.[34] The stoic self-conscious-ness, first of all, finds its abstract freedom in its perfect reclusion into the "simple essentiality of thought,"[35] entirely "turned away from the independence of things."[36] The skeptic consciousness,

and the idea that in religion there is an absolute 'being-one' of two natures at the inside of the divine being and at the inside of the believing soul" (Ibid., 153).

32  Cf. "In all of Hegel's systematic works there is one section that discusses the unhappy consciousness. [...] The unhappy one is the person who in one way or another has his ideal, the substance of his life, the plenitude of his consciousness, his essential nature, outside himself. The unhappy one is the person who is always absent from himself, never present to himself. [...] The whole territory of the unhappy consciousness is thereby ad-equately circumscribed. For this firm limitation, we thank Hegel, and now, since we are not only philosophers who view this kingdom at a distance, we shall as natives consider more closely the various stages contained therein." (Søren Kierkegaard, *Either/Or: Part I,* eds. and trans. Howard V. Hong and Edna H. Hong [Princeton: Princeton University Press, 1987], 222).

33  Wahl, *Le malheur de la conscience dans la philosophie de Hegel,* 116.

34  For a more in-depth discussion of the notion of the unhappy conscious-ness, see for instance Hyppolite, *Genesis and Structure of Hegel's Phenom-enology of Spirit,* 190–215; for Hegel's own description of the unhappy consciousness, see §§206–30 of the *Phenomenology of Spirit.*

35  Georg Wilhelm Friedrich Hegel, *Phenomenology of Spirit,* trans. A.V. Miller (Oxford: Oxford University Press, 1977), §199. In order to facilitate navigation across different editions, all references to the *Phenomenology of Spirit* are given as paragraph numbers.

36  Ibid., §200.

then, denouncing the deceptive stability and unity of stoicism, turns toward radical negation. Within this negation, however, it is doubled and becomes internally contradictory, torn apart in its unconscious confusion: "At one time it recognizes that its freedom lies in rising above all the confusion and contingency of existence, and at another time equally admits to a relapse into occupying itself with what is unessential."[37] The skeptic consciousness hence constantly moves from one extreme to the other at will, experiencing its contradictions as mere child's play. It is, as Hegel puts it, no more than "the squabbling of self-willed children."[38] Only the *unhappy* consciousness, finally, is able to acknowledge the torment that is entailed by this state of split and internal contradiction. It is "consciousness of itself as a doubled, merely contradictory being [*Wesen*],"[39] a being that is suspended in continuous oscillation between inside and outside, immanence and transcendence, singularity and universality, the finite and the infinite, this world and a world beyond, the human and the divine. The unhappy consciousness is thus haunted by an inherent restlessness; whenever "it believes itself to have achieved victory and restful unity," in one way or another, it is immediately expelled from its apparent repose.[40]

In the *Phenomenology of Spirit,* the unhappy consciousness is dialectically overcome thanks to an "actual sacrifice," the "surrender of one's own will" for the sake of a "universal will" that leads toward the realization of reason.[41] The knowledge of the absolute, or absolute knowledge, designates the direction of a final "reconciliation with itself."[42] Wahl, however, extrapolates from the moment of the unhappy consciousness and conceives

37  Ibid., §205.
38  Ibid.
39  Ibid., §206, translation modified. It is, in other words, "*for itself* the doubled consciousness of itself as self-liberating, unchangeable, and self-identical, and of itself as absolutely self-confusing and self-inverting — and it is the consciousness of this contradiction within itself."
40  Ibid., §207, translation modified.
41  Ibid., §230.
42  Ibid., §207.

of it as a universal structure of existential subjectivity (a gesture later repeated by Alexandre Kojève, who draws upon the dialectic of lord and bondsman, of master and slave, to provide a universal structure of historical human subjectivity).[43] The unhappy consciousness is thus understood, in short, as "consciousness as subject" *tout court*.[44] As Wahl puts it elsewhere, much later: "There is *only* unhappy consciousness."[45] Dialectics, then, is no guarantee for reconciliation,[46] and in this existential reading of the conditions of Hegel's rationalism, the absolute itself remains "unhappy," so to speak, internally "strained," a juxtaposition of irresolvable contradictions.[47] All hope for reconciliation is ultimately deferred to mystical experience, and it is clear that in the last instance all consciousness must remain tragic.[48]

Throughout the remainder of the century, and still today, many readers of Hegel have continued to focus on this tragic aspect of subjectivity, rejecting the idea of reconciliation and a closed system.[49] As Hyppolite noted, many of his contemporaries preferred

---

43  Cf. Alexandre Kojève, *Introduction to the Reading of Hegel: Lectures on the Phenomenology of Spirit,* ed. Allan Bloom, trans. James H. Nichols, Jr. (Ithaca: Cornell University Press, 1980).

44  Wahl, *Le malheur de la conscience dans la philosophie de Hegel,* 112.

45  Jean Wahl, *Human Existence and Transcendence,* trans. William C. Hackett (Notre Dame: University of Notre Dame Press, 2016), 54; emphasis mine.

46  Here Wahl parts ways with Hegel: Although he stresses the importance of negativity and dialectics (with Plato remaining the better dialectician as compared to Hegel), he strongly opposes the idea of a closed system and defends the role of immediacy; cf. for instance Jean Wahl, "Itinéraire ontologique," in *Les philosophes français d'aujourd'hui par eux-mêmes: Autobiographie de la philosophie française contemporaine,* eds. Gérard Deledalle and Denis Huisman (Paris: Centre de Documentation Universitaire, 1963), 58–59. For a helpful overview of Wahl's biography and work, cf. the editors' introduction "Existence, Experience, and Transcendence: An Introduction to Jean Wahl" in Jean Wahl, *Transcendence and the Concrete: Selected Writings,* eds. Alan D. Schrift and Ian Alexander Moore, 1–31 (New York: Fordham University Press, 2016).

47  Ibid., 113.

48  Ibid.

49  Cf. Bruce Baugh, *French Hegel: From Surrealism to Postmodernism* (New York: Routledge, 2003).

what Hegel calls "unhappy consciousness" to what he calls "spirit." They take up Hegel's description of self-certainty which fails to be in-itself but which, nonetheless, exists only through its transcendence toward that in-itself; but they abandon Hegel when, according to him, specific self-consciousness — subjectivity — becomes universal self-consciousness — thingness — a movement through which being is posed as subject and subject is posed as being. They accept Hegel's phenomenology but reject his ontology.[50]

As the terminology indicates, this characterization was perhaps most importantly directed at Jean-Paul Sartre, for whom, in *Being and Nothingness,* and with direct reference to Wahl (for both Hegel and Kierkegaard), the unhappy consciousness remained crucial; according to him, subjectivity is precisely a structure of perpetual unhappiness — "[h]uman reality […] is by nature an unhappy consciousness with no possibility of surpassing its unhappy state."[51] The unhappy consciousness can hence be read as an (ultimately theological) figure located at the very core of the philosophies of existence, where the "refusal of synthesis" turns it into the archetypal form of subjectivity, "a condition from which there is no escape."[52]

## *"Why not Hegel?"*

It was arguably the ubiquity of this idea of an unhappiness without escape — whether in Wahl, Sartre or Hyppolite — that provoked Deleuze's "mercilessness" toward Hegel.[53] If Hegel was, at

50  Hyppolite, *Genesis and Structure of Hegel's Phenomenology of Spirit,* 204–5.
51  Cf. Jean-Paul Sartre, *Being and Nothingness: An Essay on Phenomenological Ontology,* trans. Hazel E. Barnes (New York: Philosophical Library, 1956), 90. As a young man, Deleuze was, together with his friend Michel Tournier, an ardent reader of Sartre, and despite a certain rift he still considered him his "teacher" even in later years; cf. Deleuze, *Desert Islands,* 77–80; also cf. Giuseppe Bianco, "Deleuze before Deleuze: Humanism and Anti-Humanism (1943–1948)," forthcoming in *Critical Enquiry.*
52  Baugh, *French Hegel,* 6.
53  Cf. Deleuze, *Desert Islands,* 144.

that precise moment of his reception, a thinker of the unhappy consciousness, of negativity, of contradiction, as far as Deleuze was concerned, there could be no compromise, not even some kind of monstrous progeny, as with Kant and Bergson; Hegel remained the cypher for a philosophical "enterprise to 'burden' life" in all possible ways and "to inscribe death in life." "Somebody," Deleuze explained, "has to play the role of traitor."[54]

It is of course true that there are other important and perhaps more prominent aspects of Deleuze's rejection of Hegel and Hegelianism, including the critique of monism and the internality of relations in *Empiricism and Subjectivity* (itself adopted, by the way, from Wahl),[55] the general critique of the dialectic of opposition, contradiction, and negation in the review of Hyppolite's *Logic and Existence*,[56] the polemic against a negative conception of desire in the (Kojèvian) dialectic of master and slave in *Nietzsche and Philosophy*,[57] and the critique of infinite representation in *Difference and Repetition*.[58] And yet it can be argued that it is the interpretation of Hegelianism as a philosophy of the unhappy consciousness, although only found in a few scattered remarks, that necessitated the other critiques. From the perspective of Deleuze's ethics of affects, Hegelianism presented a particular philosophical pathology, a triumph of sad passions in thought that entailed an entire "becoming-reactive

---

54  Ibid. Regarding "monstrous" offspring, cf. Deleuze, *Negotiations,* 6.
55  Gilles Deleuze, *Empiricism and Subjectivity: An Essay on Hume's Theory of Human Nature,* trans. Constantin V. Boundas (New York: Columbia University Press, 1991). It was in this regard that Deleuze would later praise Wahl as "the one who led the reaction against the dialectic when Hegel was in full vogue at the university" (Deleuze, quoted in Dosse, *Gilles Deleuze and Félix Guattari,* 110).
56  Deleuze, *Desert Islands,* 15–18; regarding this review and its contribution to the project of an "ontology of difference," cf. Nathan Widder, "Thought after Dialectics: Deleuze's Ontology of Sense," *The Southern Journal of Philosophy* 41 (2003): 451–76.
57  Cf. Deleuze, *Nietzsche and Philosophy,* passim.
58  Deleuze, *Difference and Repetition,* 52–71; cf. also Henry Somers-Hall, *Hegel, Deleuze, and the Critique of Representation: Dialectics of Negation and Difference* (Albany: SUNY Press, 2012).

of the universe."[59] Sadness, according to Deleuze, formed the affective basis of Hegelianism and the dialectic, subtending its logic and development: "Everywhere," he claimed, "there are sad passions; the unhappy consciousness is the subject of the whole dialectic."[60]

## Sad passions: From unhappy consciousness to bad conscience

In this context, one can understand why Deleuze asserted, in *Nietzsche and Philosophy,* that "[t]he discovery dear to the dialectic is the unhappy consciousness, the deepening, the re-solution and glorification of the unhappy consciousness and its resources,"[61] even though Nietzsche himself never mentions the term. In perfect agreement with Wahl's reading, Hegel is understood as interpreting existence "from the standpoint of the unhappy consciousness," which, according to Deleuze, "is only the Hegelian version of the bad conscience."[62] Thanks to a homonymy in French, Deleuze can carry out, almost by sleight of hand, a conceptual shift from a Hegelian *conscience malheureuse* to a Nietzschean *mauvaise conscience.* Though bold, this shift is very useful for gaining a better understanding of Deleuze's critique of Hegelianism on the grounds of its "sad passions."

"Bad conscience," according to Deleuze, "is the conscience that multiplies its pain," the conscience "which has found a technique for manufacturing pain by turning active force back against itself: the squalid workshop," or the workshop, one might add, of the labor of the negative.[63] It is an apparatus for the production of a particular form of subjectivity, the unhappy consciousness, which in turn implies a specific invention, the invention of a "*new sense,*" "*an internal sense, an inward sense.*"[64] This sense, as that of an abyss, an irreducible tension at the core

59  Deleuze, *Nietzsche and Philosophy,* 196.
60  Ibid.
61  Ibid., 159.
62  Ibid., 19, 132.
63  Ibid., 129.
64  Ibid.

of the subject, is ultimately a sense for pain, its "multiplication" and "internalization."[65] As Hegel wrote, the unhappy consciousness (or in fact self-consciousness as such) is "only the *pain* or *grief* of Spirit that struggles, but without success, out towards objectivity."[66] And while Hegel, once again, conceived of this pain, this grief, this suffering, as no more than a passing stage in the (auto-)biography of spirit, after Wahl it remained the unsurpassable internal tension or contradiction that formed the condition of all subjectivity.

For Deleuze, this form of subjectivity, constituted at the surface of a strange economy of sad passions in which "pain is healed by manufacturing yet more pain, by internalizing it still further," remains invariably passive, even reactive, constantly slipping toward the inaction of *ressentiment*.[67] The unhappy consciousness, part and parcel, then, of a genealogy of morality, seems utterly "powerless to create new ways of thinking and feeling" — with the exception, of course, of new forms of pain and ways of suffering.[68] Wallowing in its despair, its suspension between the singular and the universal, it cannot but perpetually encounter itself as an other, and an other as itself; its basic structure is constituted by "bad encounters" with itself and/as an other, as something that "do[es] not agree with it and tend[s] to decompose it, to destroy it."[69] What results is the existential despair of an existence that is *essentially* painful.

At this point, Deleuze's anti-Hegelian Nietzsche merges with his somewhat peculiar Spinoza,[70] and it becomes clear that he studies the unhappy consciousness — and with it the (quite abstract) whole of Hegelianism — from an ethical perspective,

65  Ibid., 132.

66  Hegel, *Phenomenology of Spirit,* §673, trans. modified.

67  Deleuze, *Nietzsche and Philosophy,* 130. Deleuze refers to Friedrich Nietzsche, *Genealogy of Morals,* III.15.

68  Ibid., 159.

69  Gilles Deleuze, *Spinoza: Practical Philosophy,* trans. Robert Hurley (San Francisco: City Lights Books, 1988), 100.

70  Cf. ibid., 17, where Deleuze speaks of Spinoza's "major resemblances with Nietzsche."

which boils down to a generalized ethology that is predominantly interested in "the compositions of relations or capacities between different things,"[71] their collective "capacities for affecting and being affected," in short: their power of acting.[72] Unhappiness, and this has been implicit throughout the present text, is here treated as synonymous with sadness, and sadness, according to Spinoza and Deleuze, is nothing other than "the diminution of the power of acting."[73] Within the dual framework of a philosophical symptomatology and an ethics of affects, then, Hegelianism appears as a clinical case. A movement ostensibly based on the irreducible unhappiness of an individual consciousness, an existential ontology rooted in sad passions, is considered inherently incapacitating; "sad passions," Deleuze declares, "always amount to impotence."[74]

This impotence, moreover, a pathology that testifies to the subjection to a reign of sad passions, a reign of the negative, has political implications. "There is no unhappy consciousness which is not also man's enslavement"[75]:

Everything that involves sadness serves tyranny and oppression. Everything that involves sadness must be denounced as bad, as something that separates us from our power of acting: not only remorse and guilt, not only meditation on death, but even hope, even security, which signify powerlessness.[76]

From Deleuze's point of view, a philosophy, an ethics, a life based on the sad passions of the unhappy consciousness was tantamount to a form of death and had to be avoided and re-

---

71  Deleuze, *Spinoza: Practical Philosophy,* 126.

72  Ibid., 124.

73  Ibid., 50. Cf. also Gilles Deleuze, *Expressionism in Philosophy: Spinoza,* trans. Martin Joughin (New York: Zone Books, 1990), 274.

74  Ibid., 28.

75  Deleuze, *Nietzsche and Philosophy,* 190.

76  Deleuze, *Spinoza: Practical Philosophy,* 72. Deleuze refers to Baruch Spinoza, *Ethics,* IV.P67 and IV.P47; cf. also Deleuze, *Expressionism in Philosophy,* 270.

sisted. Hegelianism became the target of his polemic precisely because it was presented as a "monstrous enterprise to submit life to negativity, the enterprise of *ressentiment* and unhappy consciousness."[77] His own philosophical enterprise, on the other hand, was thus committed to learning how not to fall prey, as so many of his contemporaries did, to such a "philosophy of death," as Kojève called it,[78] a form of metaphysical melancholia due to which "[o]ur power is immobilized, and can no longer do anything but react."[79]

*Joyful passions*

Accordingly, Deleuze, as mentioned before, sought to propose a vital and affirmative conception of philosophy. Philosophers, like artists, had to be "civilization's doctors," according to Nietzsche,[80] and hence it was their task to find, to invent a remedy for an unhappy philosophy based on sad passions inhibiting action. This remedy was of course a philosophy of joyful passions that catalyzed action. If sadness was "the diminution of the power of acting," joy had to be, according to another Spinozist formulation, "the increase of the power of acting." For Deleuze, therefore, "only joy is worthwhile, joy remains, bringing us near to action, and to the bliss of action."[81] It should be clarified, however, that this joy is the joy of association, always transversal, the joy of becoming as opposed to the sadness of being (which is ultimately the sadness of the *impossibility of mere being*). Within Deleuze's Spinozist and Nietzschean "clinic," a joyful existence hence presents an antidote to the apparent sickness and sadness of the dialectic and the unhappy consciousness. It is only by vir-

---

77  Deleuze, *Desert Islands,* 144, translation modified.
78  Alexandre Kojève, *Introduction à la lecture de Hegel: Leçons sur la Phéno-ménologie de l'Esprit professées de 1933 à 1939 à l'École des Hautes Études,* ed. Raymond Queneau (Paris: Gallimard, 1947), 539. The shortened English translation does not contain this expression.
79  Deleuze, *Spinoza: Practical Philosophy,* 101.
80  Deleuze, *Negotiations,* 141.
81  Deleuze, *Spinoza: Practical Philosophy,* 28.

tue of joyful passions that "our power expands, compounds with the power of the other, and unites with the loved object;"[82] because of joyful passions we might eventually pass from passion to action, and only then can "we ourselves become causes of our own affects and masters of our adequate perceptions," only then will "our body [gain] access to the power of acting, and our mind to the power of comprehending, which is its way of acting."[83] Joy, in this specific sense, is presented as a way out of the sadness of enslavement, out of the enslavement of sadness.

Deleuze's critique of the unhappy consciousness and of Hegelianism more generally is therefore, once again, not at all a purely theoretical endeavor. It is a particular and historically specific intervention regarding the way in which philosophy is *practiced*. Philosophy, according to Deleuze, should never be a mournful matter of contradiction and negation, lost in the circuits of representation. If the philosophy of French mid-century Hegelianism was, according to Foucault, "presented as the way to achieve a rational understanding of the tragic as it was experienced by the generation immediately preceding ours, and still threatening for our own," the new philosophy sought after by Deleuze was to be a joyful concern, a "gay science," to use Nietzsche's term, a question of life, of affirmation and of difference.[84] But this particular intervention on behalf of a different philosophy (a philosophy of difference) was also rooted in a particular conception of ethics. For Deleuze, thought and speculation were, despite their indisputable autonomy, inseparable from the milieu that provided their conditions on the one hand and the habitat that they shaped on the other. Therefore, the great question regarding the operations of philosophy had to be posed in terms of ethics as ethology, and was, in this sense,

82  Ibid., 101. Deleuze refers to Spinoza, *Ethics,* iv.P18.

83  Ibid., 104.

84  Cf. Deleuze, *Difference and Repetition,* xxi: "The time is coming when it will hardly be possible to write a book of philosophy as it has been done for so long: 'Ah! the old style…' The search for new means of philosophical expression was begun by Nietzsche and must be pursued today in relation to the renewal of certain other arts, such as the theatre or the cinema."

also a pragmatic question.[85] Even when it came to an allegedly
theoretical practice like philosophy, Deleuze was at least implicitly concerned with its non- and meta-philosophical implications, with what it enables to do and what it prevents from
doing. Philosophy was thus conceived not as the guardian of a
truth given in advance (for instance the truth of reconciliation
or of its impossibility), but as a field of experimentation and of
the production of new powers (Spinoza), values (Nietzsche), or
forms of life (Foucault). "*Concepts* are inseparable from *affects,*
i.e., from the powerful effects they exert on our life, and *percepts,* i.e., the new ways of seeing or perceiving they provoke in
us."[86] This phrase, though taken from a much later text, reaches
to the very core of Deleuze's philosophy of philosophy, and it
is from this point of view that one can understand the critique
of Hegelianism throughout his work. His philosophical argu-
ments against Hegel, whether directed against monism and
internal relations, against negativity and contradiction, against
the dialectic of master and slave, against infinite representation,
or finally, as in this case, against the unhappy consciousness,
formed part of a resistance against the implicit and explicit politics and ethics (or morality) of a particular Hegelian philosophy.
For Deleuze, they were part of a search for a different form of
life, a form of life that refuses to let itself be closed in, a form
of life shaped through an affirmation of difference. Hence the
"practical problem" that Deleuze identified when distinguishing Spinoza's *Ethics* from a morality: "*How does one arrive at a
maximum of joyful passions?,* proceeding from there to free and
active feelings (although our place in Nature seems to condemn

85  On the relation between speculation and practice in Deleuze's philosophy,
    cf. Sjoerd van Tuinen, "Deleuze: Speculative and Practical Philosophy," in
    *Genealogies of Speculation: Materialism and Subjectivity since Structural-
    ism,* eds. Armen Avanessian and Suhail Malik, 93–114 (London: Blooms-
    bury, 2016).
86  Gilles Deleuze, *Two Regimes of Madness: Texts and Interviews 1975–1995,*
    ed. David Lapoujade, trans. Ames Hodges and Michael Taormina (New
    York: MIT Press, 2006), 238.

us to bad encounters and sadnesses)."[87] The world may indeed be full of tensions, as Wahl asserted with the young Hegel, or full of forces, but those must be thought outside of the ultimately representational logic of sadness in order to be made creative. Like art and life, philosophy, for Deleuze, was a matter of experimentation and creation, of the creation of concepts of course, but also of joyful passions.

87  Deleuze, *Spinoza: Practical Philosophy,* 28.

# 2

# To Have Done with Judgment of "Reason": Deleuze's Aesthetic Ontology

*Samantha Bankston*

Friedrich Nietzsche, in "'Reason' in Philosophy" from *Twilight of the Idols,* alerts us to the pitfalls of a metaphysical history that grounds itself on a fundamental error of temporality:

> Change, mutation, becoming in general were formerly taken as proof of appearance, as a sign of the presence of something which led us astray. Today, on the contrary, we see ourselves as it were entangled in error, *necessitated* to error, to precisely the extent that our prejudice in favor of reason compels us to posit unity, identity, duration, substance, cause, materiality, being; however sure we may be, on the basis of a strict reckoning, *that* error is to be found here.[1]

These errors of Reason — unity, identity, mechanistic causality, and permanence — erect a tradition of judgment in the history of philosophy. The fundamental error of Reason is temporal in nature, where discontinuous states of Being supplant continuous processes of becoming. For Nietzsche, this amounts to a subordination of sense to a moralistic framework that never shakes

1   Friedrich Nietzsche, *Twilight of the Idols,* trans. Michael Tanner (London: Penguin Classics, 1990), 47.

off the onto-theological hangover of the Ancient Greeks, save Heraclitus.[2] Reason in the history of philosophy is a mortification of thought — concepts are lifeless artifacts of the past. If we eradicate Reason from philosophy, then what are we doing? As Gilles Deleuze exclaims, "We're looking for 'vitality.'"[3] Deleuze takes seriously the errors of Reason, as outlined by Nietzsche, and rather than do away with metaphysics, he shatters the pillars of Reason with his critique of the dogmatic "image of thought." Just as the Signifier dies along with God, judgment in philosophy dies along with Reason. In this essay, I will illuminate the concept of becoming that Deleuze uses to reconfigure the history of metaphysics along the lines of Nietzsche's critique of Reason. As the temporal logic of becoming in Deleuze splits into the becoming of pure events and the becoming of sensation, a philosophy of affects corrects the errors which arose from Reason. Ultimately, Deleuze creates a metaphysical system beyond good and evil, replacing the dogmatic errors of Reason with the aesthetic potential of the new.

Using the centrifugal force of the eternal return of difference, Deleuze's philosophical collage of the likes of Spinoza, Hume, Leibniz, Borges, Proust, Bergson, Simondon, Duns Scotus, and others forms a universe of immanence that is at base a metaphysical system in concert with Nietzsche's thought. The positive formulation of Nietzsche's critique of Reason is a pre-individual world of affects where all identities are merely an effect of the unconditioned flux of force. In the beautiful aphorism that closes *The Will to Power,* Nietzsche depicts his anti-philosophical world at odds with the history of metaphysics. When he asks,

2   "Philosophy in the only way I still allow it to stand, as the most general form of history, as an attempt somehow to describe Heraclitean becoming and to abbreviate it into signs (so to speak, to translate and mummify it into a kind of illusory being)." Friedrich Nietzsche, *Writings from the Late Notebooks,* ed. Rüdiger Bittner, trans. Kate Sturge (Cambridge: Cambridge University Press, 2003), 26.

3   Gilles Deleuze, *Desert Islands and Other Texts: 1953–1974,* ed. David Lapoujade, trans. Michael Taormina (Los Angeles: Semiotext(e), 2004), 142.

"And do you know what 'the world' is to me?"[4] we discover a play of forces in contradiction, both one and many, perpetually in-between, and eternally recurring without a goal but the act of recurrence itself.

Nietzsche begins the description of his Dionysian world with an "AND," where the power of the false breaks with the logic of identity, the principle of sufficient reason, the law of excluded middle, and the law of non-contradiction. Furthermore, negation and nothingness play no role in Nietzsche's world, for all forms, structures, institutions, and things are undone through the eternal return of difference and the unhinging of efficient, formal, material, and final causation. Pre-subjective forces form multiplicities that are always in-between, "anchoring" all individuation in chaotic flux, painting an aesthetic ontology of pure intensities beyond the reifying logic of Reason. After Nietzsche, it becomes unthinkable to do metaphysics in the same way. To invent a new and rigorous metaphysics requires the elaboration of a complex set of processes and (anti-)logic that systematizes all of the features of Nietzsche's Dionysian world without resorting to mechanisms of transcendence, and this is precisely what Deleuze accomplishes. The first step in developing a new image of thought is holding all processes to the light of becoming, to maintain the primacy of the unconditioned as the driving force of a new metaphysics.

When Deleuze attacks the four shackles of representational thought (analogy, opposition, resemblance, and identity), he simultaneously opens the way for an alternative image of thought. Each of the shackles can be traced to a fundamental temporal error: the attempt to conceive of change as a structural derivative of the immutable. Henri Bergson and Nietzsche converge on the criticism of mechanistic causality and its employment of "reason" to freeze pure flux in order to construct an image of becoming. Deleuze connects these criticisms and asks how

4   Friedrich Nietzsche, *The Will to Power,* ed. Walter Kaufmann, trans. Walter Kaufmann and Reginald J. Hollingdale (New York: Random House, 1967), 549–50.

a counter-causal process appropriate to the concept of becoming might be created. Of the list of errors in reason provided by Nietzsche: unity is replaced by multiplicity; identity is replaced by difference, while essences are replaced by assemblages or haecceities; duration (which means something akin to permanence for Nietzsche) is replaced by instantaneity; substance is replaced by virtual relation; mechanistic causality is replaced by quasi-causality; materiality is replaced by intensity; and, throwing all the features of this new anti-reason in motion: being is replaced by becoming.[5]

In accordance with Nietzsche's critique of Reason, Deleuze enlists artists and philosophers who shake the very foundation of a philosophical history which is plagued by temporal distortion. In "On Nietzsche and the Image of Thought" he states, "Hume, Bergson, and Proust interest me so much because in their work can be found profound elements for a new image of thought. There's something extraordinary in the way they tell us: thinking means something else than what you believe."[6] All of the thinkers invoked in Deleuze's revolutionary image of thought radically rethink temporality. They agree that Understanding cannot produce an encounter with becoming — it is only through encounters in sensation that we are thrown into its chaotic flux. In Deleuze's temporal collage, David Hume provides the system of relations arising from a new image of thought; this is the principle of exteriority, which encourages the conjunctive proliferation of pre-individual intensities below the logic of the Same seen in re-presentation. In this revised, pre-individual, nomadic image of thought Deleuze announces the pitfalls of representation and its reified structure of time, and categorical conditions are cast aside in favor of an exploration of the unconditioned. The reading that Deleuze gives to Nietzsche's philosophical project in the following passage can also be applied to Deleuze: "For Nietzsche, it is about getting something through in every past, present, and future code,

5    Ibid.
6    Deleuze, *Desert Islands,* 139.

something which does not and will not let itself be recoded."[7] That which repeats throughout past, present, and future, yet escapes all coding, is difference, the new, in short: becoming.

Nietzsche's Dionysian world directly contends with Reason and the use of judgment in representational Being. In *Difference and Repetition,* the categorical application of judgment is decried through its two uses of distribution and hierarchization. Distribution partitions concepts through the use of common sense, hierarchization measures subjects through primary or good sense.[8] Difference is neutralized through categorical distribution, and all categorical thought — that of Aristotle, Kant, and even Hegel — implies the philosophy of judgment. Subsequently, it is impossible to think of the unconditioned, or the uncoded, when employing judgment, since judgment retains identity in the concept by using analogy to relate to being.[9] The error in judgment emerges from the immobilizing mechanisms of chronological, homogeneous time, which reifies becoming in an attempt to categorize it. Consequently, an aesthetic ontology is needed to counter the categorical logic of judgment, and this is accomplished through the construction of a concept of becoming that deploys the generative "both/and" in its process of individuation.

Deleuze's concept of becoming is pivotal to his metaphysics, yet it is often misunderstood or invoked in a vague sense that conflates its divergent processes. Mapping "becoming" across Deleuze's works involves wading through terminological variance (e.g., becoming, difference, becomings, Aion, becoming-mad, becoming-woman, eternal return of difference, becoming-imperceptible, blocs of becoming), tracking the regional logics that form the ontological neighborhoods in his texts, and tracking the points of convergence between being and time. With respect to the latter, Deleuze's thought pushes ontology to the

---

7    Ibid., 253.
8    Gilles Deleuze, *Difference and Repetition,* trans. Paul Patton (New York: Columbia University Press, 1994), 33.
9    Ibid.

limit, even farther than Martin Heidegger, causing the distinction between ontology and temporality to collapse. This collapse is admitted outright by Deleuze in an interview with Jean-Noël Vuarnet: "Yes, I finished the book — on repetition and difference (they're the same thing) as the actual categories of our thought."[10] In an ontology premised by absolute becoming, that which was an "is" necessarily becomes an "and," becomes temporality itself.

In other work[11] I have delineated Deleuze's revolutionary notion of becoming as it deploys two divergent modes of becoming, which he hints at in *What Is Philosophy?*: sensory becoming and absolute becoming, the latter Deleuze and Félix Guattari term "conceptual becoming."[12] Sensory becoming falls under an umbrella of terms throughout his canon: at the beginning of his career his use of sensory becoming is often referred to simply as "becoming," and later it is known as "becomings," "*a* becoming," "becoming-mad," "sensory-bloc," and so on. Having mapped the processes of becoming across Deleuze's works, the double nature of becoming is made clear. Not only is every instant distributed into the opposing streams of the past and the future, there are two distinct modes of becoming at work in Deleuze's ontology.

Sensory becoming functions through what he calls "a molecular memory, but as a factor of integration into a majoritarian or molar system."[13] This mode of becoming pertains to sensation, and is an appropriation of late Bergsonian duration (duration without consciousness), yet endowed with the telescoping power of sensation witnessed in Proustian reminiscence. Deleuze

10  Deleuze, *Desert Islands,* 142, emphasis in original.
11  Samantha Bankston, *Deleuze and Becoming(s)* (London: Bloomsbury Publications, 2015).
12  Gilles Deleuze and Félix Guattari, *What Is Philosophy?,* trans. Hugh Tomlinson and Graham Burchell (New York: Columbia University Press, 1994), 177.
13  Gilles Deleuze and Félix Guattari, *A Thousand Plateaus: Capitalism and Schizophrenia,* trans. Brian Massumi (Minneapolis: University of Minnesota Press, 1987), 294.

follows Bergson in distinguishing duration from becoming. In *Bergsonism,* Deleuze notes that duration is a mode of becoming when he states that duration is "a becoming that endures, a change that is substance itself."[14] By combining an enduring becoming and substance, Deleuze redefines the materiality of the present according to the Bergsonian model of internal change, and consequently, he redefines substance as a *relationship* in the process of becoming; substance is replaced by intensive process in materiality. Thus through Bergsonian duration, or what later is termed sensory becoming, Deleuze replaces the notion of substance with the self-differing relation. Not only is becoming the vehicle that produces what we perceive as substance in the lived present, but Deleuze also leaves us a clue pertaining to the multiplicity of the concept of becoming by writing "*a* becoming."[15] This mode of becoming subverts the chronological present by retaining a molecular memory that disorients all organization, and forms blocs of coexistence within sensation. Sensory becoming is a virtual multiplicity that expresses the logic of assemblages. In other words, it is the subversive temporality of the depth of bodies. For Deleuze, duration signifies the ontological memory of the pure past. In the chapter entitled "1730: Becoming-Intense, Becoming-Animal, Becoming-Imperceptible" in *A Thousand Plateaus,* Deleuze and Guattari prankishly interpose "memory" and "becoming," and then they reveal that "[w]herever we used the word 'memories' in the preceding pages, we were wrong to do so; we meant to say 'becoming,' we were saying becoming."[16] This intentional erasure distinguishes molar from molecular memory. Sensory becoming is not anti-memory, only anti-molar-memory. Becomings endure, cohering through ontological memory, which is at the level of the molecular. The individuating process of ontological memory — the memory of becomings — is expressed by Deleuze in terms of Proustian

---

14 Gilles Deleuze, *Bergsonism,* trans. Hugh Tomlinson and Barbara Habberjam (New York: Zone Books, 1991), 37.

15 Emphasis is mine.

16 Deleuze and Guattari, *A Thousand Plateaus,* 294.

reminiscence and is a supplemental entrance into Bergson's and Marcel Proust's notion of the pure past. Deleuze writes, "to remember is to create, is *to reach that point where the associative chain breaks, leaps over the constituted individual, is transferred to the birth of an individuating world.*"[17] The process of creation that arises from ontological memory is the code breaking logic (or "antilogos") of sensory becoming whose molecular durations ignite individuation beneath the representation of entities, subjects, and objects. This is not the memory of a molar subject, one constructed by an act of re-presentation. Opposed to what he calls "molar subjects," the differenciated becoming in sensation is a pre-subjective molecular collectivity and is consistent with Deleuze's re-appropriation of the multiplicity of duration.[18] When Deleuze speaks in terms of *a* becoming, or becomings, he is speaking of a concept of becoming that unfolds serially along the points of molecular duration. As opposed to sensory becoming, absolute becoming is the immaterial mode of becoming, the eternal return of difference. As was the case with sensory becoming, absolute becoming is subject to terminological variance across Deleuze's works. The most common formulations of the concept appear as either "the eternal return," "the pure and empty form of time," or "Aion." The temporal logic of absolute becoming differs in kind from sensory becoming precisely on the axis of memory.

When developing the notion of the eternal return, Deleuze explains that it is the being of becoming. He, of course, does not mean Being, as understood in Nietzsche's errors of Reason,

17  Gilles Deleuze, *Proust and Signs,* trans. Richard Howard (Minneapolis: University of Minnesota Press, 2000), 111.

18  Deleuze and Guattari, *A Thousand Plateaus,* 275. Sensory becoming involves a molecular composition that defies the effectuated causality of representation. Molecular becoming is connected to the "pathology of duration," whereby the relationship established between two things encourages the exchange of their intensive features, or their molecules. "Yes, all becomings are molecular: the animal, flower, or stone one becomes are molecular collectivities, haecceities, not molar subjects, objects, or form that we know from the outside and recognize from experience, through science, or by habit."

but something else entirely. For Deleuze and Nietzsche, Being is overturned by becoming, and the eternal return is the uncoded virtual relation that is in-between being. Throughout Deleuze's works, but particularly in *Nietzsche and Philosophy*, it is clear that what returns is the act of returning itself. The eternal return as the pure and empty form of time is the being of becoming, fusing temporality and ontology. Deleuze himself remarks, "As we have seen, the condition of the action by default does not return; the condition of the agent by metamorphosis does not return; all that returns, the eternal return, is the *unconditioned* in the product."[19] The unconditioned in the product is not itself a product; instead of being static, it is the differential relation and pure process. Furthermore, it is the selectivity of the eternal return that keeps the first two syntheses, present and past, from returning. Building upon his elaboration of the eternal return in *Difference and Repetition*, Deleuze describes absolute becoming in *Desert Islands* as follows:

> It is the law of a world without being, without unity, without identity. Far from *presupposing* the One or the Same, the eternal return constitutes the only unity of the multiple as such, the only identity of what differs: coming back is the only "being" of becomings.[20]

Thus, absolute becoming fractures identity, substance, permanence, and materiality along Nietzsche's Dionysian lines. Nothing that existed in actual form returns in the third synthesis of time: the future — neither partially nor wholly. All associative chains of memory break, enacting a repetition of ontological forgetting.

Deleuze accentuates the necessity of active forgetting in the dissolution of identities through absolute becoming. He takes note of Pierre Klossowski's interpretation of the eternal return,

19  Deleuze, *Difference and Repetition,* 297.
20  Deleuze, *Desert Islands,* 124.

which moves from the act of willing to becoming-other.[21] The chain of duration (molecular memory) is broken through the movement of the eternal return, which is the dissimulation of absolute becoming. Deleuze implicates the forgetfulness of absolute becoming when he states that the eternal return constitutes the only unity of the world in its repetition and is "the only identity of a world which has no 'same' at all except through repetition."[22] He agrees with Klossowski's (and Michel Foucault's) assessment that the death of God necessarily implies the death of the self, which is revealed through the active forgetfulness of becoming. The dissolution of identities ignites the break of durational becoming through active forgetfulness at the ontological level. Ontological forgetfulness is not restricted to consciousness, or to the selectivity of thought, but is an integral aspect of becoming. Klossowski claims that "[f]orgetting thus raises eternal becoming and the absorption of all identity to the level of being."[23] The forgetfulness of becoming is a necessary condition for the enactment of the eternal return, as well as its dissolution of forms and identities. Deleuze appropriates the representational forgetfulness on the surface level of forgetting in Klossowski and injects it into the pre-individual movement of absolute becoming. The ontological forgetfulness of absolute becoming mimics Nietzsche's call toward active forgetting in the affirmative creation of the future.

21  The following passage on Klossowski demonstrates the confluence of the will to power and the eternal return as effectively undoing the opposition between the one and the many. The connection to willing and becoming-other reappears in Deleuze's ontology as the relationship between the manifest levels of the eternal return in willing and the latent levels of the return in pre-subjective chaos. "It is in this sense that Mr. Klossowski wanted to show us a world of intense fluctuations in the Will to power, where identities are lost, and where each one cannot want itself without wanting all the other possibilities, without becoming innumerable 'others,' without apprehending itself as a fortuitous moment, whose very chance implies the necessity of the whole series" (ibid., 122).

22  Ibid., 123.

23  Pierre Klossowski, "Nietzsche's Experience of the Eternal Return," in *The New Nietzsche,* ed. David B. Allison, 107–20 (Cambridge: MIT Press, 1985), 108.

In addition to its primordial features of active forgetting and selectivity of being, Deleuze formulates absolute becoming (or the eternal return) in terms of intensive quantity. Rejecting interpretations of Nietzsche that ascribe purely qualitative readings to force, Deleuze posits a notion of intensive quantity as early as *Nietzsche and Philosophy*. Rather than forfeit quantity to chronometric homogeneous measure, he argues for the existence of intensive quantity in Nietzsche's thought. Thus absolute becoming is understood to be the differential relation of intensive quantities. A theory of intensive quantity installs a precise mathematical model into the notion of force in Nietzsche's philosophy. Whenever Nietzsche criticizes the tendency of science to reduce qualitative difference to extensive quantities of equal measure, he is calling for an understanding of force as quantitative difference. Qualitative difference always includes a quantitative difference, and this notion of intensive quantitative difference is central to Deleuze's theory of absolute becoming: "Difference in quantity is the essence of force and of the relation of force to force."[24] Conceiving of difference through processes of intensive quantity opens up a theory of becoming that is premised on relations and not fixed terms. This is the point at which Deleuze enlists Gottfried Wilhelm Leibniz into his elaboration of absolute becoming. He restructures the Leibnizian calculus through processes of immanence and thus provides a foundation for a quantitative theory of absolute becoming, using a revised theory of Nietzschean force. Because Deleuze articulates this force as intensive quantity, he is able to plug intensities into differential equations, restructuring the concept of becoming — both sensory and absolute — through the infinitesimal calculus. In Deleuze's Leibniz, transcendence and harmony are replaced with immanence and chaos, thus deploying the power of the false, whereby Deleuze provides a Nietzschean reading of Leibniz via Jorge Luis Borges. Where incompossibilities are able to exist in the same world, virtually, the eternal return of

---

24  Gilles Deleuze, *Nietzsche and Philosophy,* trans. Hugh Tomlinson (New York: Columbia University Press, 2006), 43.

absolute becoming produces a garden of forking paths. Borges' "The Garden of Forking Paths," where the protagonist is able to activate infinite unselected potential futures that exist in the virtual realm simultaneously, serves as a model of incompossible lines of becoming, or divergent syntheses of time.[25] Absolute becoming is the process of bifurcation that splits the past and the future, causing time to fork virtually, simultaneously subverting the chronological present in a mad process of material becoming in sensation.

In terms of Deleuze's appropriation of Leibniz's infinitesimal calculus, absolute becoming refers to the differential relation, while sensory becoming refers to the integration. As Simon Duffy explains, integration is not only the summation of differentials, but also the inverse of the differential relation.[26] In a stroke of brilliance, Deleuze formulates both modes of becoming as inversions of one another with respect to Leibniz's differential calculus. Absolute becoming as the model of the differential relation has zero duration and is the paradoxical sidestepping of the present in its nomadic distribution of singularities throughout the virtual. Meanwhile, sensory becoming is the model of integration, the summation of differentials of molecular memory in sensation. The question then arises as to how these two ontological mirrors interact, what are the virtual processes that connect them? Clearly, any form of causality elaborated in the history of metaphysics will be inadequate to a purely immanent ontology. Instead of dismissing causality as an illusory production in representational thought that expels difference, Deleuze seeks to reconstruct causality according to the heterogeneous features of becoming.[27] He elaborates his theory

25  Jorge Luis Borges, "The Garden of Forking Paths," in *Labyrinths*, trans. Donald A. Yates (New York: New Directions Publishing, 2007), 19–29.

26  Simon Duffy, "The Logic of Expression in Deleuze's Expressionism and Philosophy: Spinoza: A Strategy of Engagement," *International Journal of Philosophical Studies* 12, no. 1 (March 2004): 47–60.

27  Friedrich Nietzsche, *The Gay Science: With a Prelude in Rhymes and an Appendix of Songs,* trans. Walter Kaufmann (New York: Vintage Books, 1974), 172. In this sense, Deleuze's innovative counter-effectuating causality

of quasi-causality in *The Logic of Sense,* and the notion hardly appears elsewhere. The quasi-cause is the untimely operator between absolute becoming of the eternal return and sensory becoming of molecular memory. Quasi-causality differs from other forms of causality in its distributive power of difference and its ability to create an ultimate divide between the cause and the effect. It does not function along the lines of material, formal, efficient, or final causes. Furthermore, as pointed out by Daniel W. Smith, quasi-causality differs from the medieval categories of emanative and transitive causalities.[28] Deleuze borrows the notion of immanent causation from Spinoza, but maintains a Nietzschean critique of substance in the process. Smith explains this appropriation when he says,

> In Spinoza's immanent causality, not only does the cause remain in itself, but its effect remains "immanate" within it, rather than emanating from it. The effect (mode) remains in its cause no less than the cause remains in itself (substance).[29]

However, as Smith points out, Deleuze eliminates Spinoza's substance, making ontology purely modal. A modal, or differential, world forces Deleuze to re-conceptualize the content of immanent causation. Since there is no God, no transcendental signifier, difference is immanent to the cause itself, which results in

can be seen as a tribute to Nietzsche. Deleuze reconstructs causality to correct the criticisms launched by Nietzsche. The imagistic construction of causality, and its elimination of difference and becoming, is absorbed into an anti-causal causality in Deleuze. Nietzsche ruthlessly critiqued the retroactive projection of cause and effect into the flux of nature. We see this salient criticism often in his works, particularly in *The Gay Science.* "We have uncovered a manifold one-after-another where the naïve man and inquirer of older cultures only saw two separate things 'Cause' and 'effect' is what one says; but we have merely perfected the image of becoming without reaching beyond the image or behind it."

28  Daniel W. Smith, "The Doctrine of Univocity: Deleuze's ontology of immanence," in *Deleuze and Religion,* ed. Mary Briden, 167–83 (London: Routledge, 2001).

29  Ibid., 174.

a distributive destruction of the logic of identity. Deleuze paints a universe that repeats the unconditioned of the cause in the effect when he eliminates all transcendence in immanent causation. As he explains, "The autonomy of the effect is thus defined initially by its difference in nature from the cause; in the second place, it is defined by its relation to the quasi-cause."[30] The effect is synonymous with the event and is bestowed full autonomy by the operation of the counter-causal process. There are no longer real causes in the virtual, only effects. As the effect differs in kind from corporeal bodies in mixture, it is independent of the cause in the classical sense and is impenetrable, impassive, neutral, and devoid of qualitative distinction. Despite the impassibility of events (also called singularities, extraordinary points of inflection), they perpetually resonate with other events through the series of effects produced in the nexus of becoming. The paradoxical series, or lines, proliferated through the absolute becoming of Aion, fragment the separation between past and future, where the quasi-cause nomadically distributes singularities in no fewer than two temporal series.

In an attempt at speculation, Deleuze presents the inner mechanics of a virtual, immanent plane as the resonance of diverging and converging series produced through the proliferating force of becoming. The quasi-cause illuminates a system connected through difference. Events do not have external causes, and they communicate not through admixture but through the differential distribution of nomadic singularities. Deleuze's complex concept of quasi-causality retains the Dionysian world of sensation and rejects the immobilizing categories of Being. All relations occur externally through the operation of the quasi-cause, rather than internally, which would lead to the static mechanism inherent to the logic of identity.

As such, the quasi-cause extracts singularities from the passing present and distributes them in a double movement that

30  Gilles Deleuze, *The Logic of Sense,* ed. Constantin V. Boundas, trans. Mark Lester and Charles Stivale (New York: Columbia University Press, 1990), 95.

constructs events. Since absolute becoming functions according to the logic of the paradoxical instant — the self-eluding moment that is never present — it is simultaneously more contracted than the smallest unit of actual time and more elongated than the entire circle of actuality. The present instantaneously gives rise to the event, and the truth of the event doubles — as a phantasm of the broken present (the past), and as the constellation of singularities that may be actualized in the present (the future). That is not to say that the event, once actualized, resembles its virtual counterpart, but rather that its movement is automatically doubled in the extracting moment of the quasi-cause. Deleuze remarks on the distancing mechanism of the quasi-cause when he writes,

> But the event nonetheless retains an eternal truth upon the line of the Aion, which divides it eternally into a proximate past and an imminent future. The Aion endlessly subdivides the event and pushes away past as well as future, without ever rendering them less urgent.[31]

It is important to recall that the pure event *never* happens but is a confluence of forces, or jets of singularities that are perpetually displaced by the instantaneous machine of becoming. The garden of forking paths in Borges serves as a model for the line of Aion. Eternally proliferating incompossible series continue to fork as the empty form of time: the future. Depending upon the neighborhoods of proximity, one may initiate a line of flight that activates, say, a Karl Marx effect, which is actualized in a way that was never actually lived by Marx himself. The individuation of singularities along the line of Aion informs actual effects, which in turn reorients their virtual counterparts. The genesis of virtual events is static, as it divests all singularities of memory trace, while the virtual relations in sensation are characterized by a spatiotemporal dynamism of molecular duration. Meanwhile, both modes of becoming contingently destabilize

31  Ibid., 63.

individuated forms in the actual. And although Deleuze and Guattari focus more on the depth of bodies, or sensory becoming, in *A Thousand Plateaus,* it is essential to understand the integral relationship between the becoming of events, or what they will later discuss as "conceptual becoming," and the becoming of sense. Too often, these two divergent processes of becoming are conflated in the secondary literature, which results in an "otherworldly" misreading of Deleuze. This very conflation is the central error in both Slavoj Žižek's and Alain Badiou's mischaracterization of Deleuze as a philosopher of the One. The absence of negation and lack does not result in monism. The processes of becoming diverge, whether they involve sensation or concepts, and although absolute flux applies to both, this plays out in vastly different ways. Think of the ritornello, a concept invented by Deleuze and Guattari, which is the eternal return oriented toward sensation, where baroque whirls and folds repeat as a matter of expression. Therefore, in sensation, the Nietzschean world of intensities unfettered by causal relations is maintained. Nietzsche's disavowal of "causality" is also metaphysically maintained in absolute becoming, the appropriation of Nietzsche's eternal return for the sake of difference. The two opposing temporal features of memory and forgetting are different tendencies of the same concept of becoming, since becoming is a multiplicity that corresponds to the plane upon which it is operating. In the realm of materiality we have the subversive sensory becoming of ontological memory; in the realm of ideas we have absolute becoming of ontological forgetting, yet the two are inexorably co-generative.

Deleuze makes forgetfulness ontological by posing it against the category of negation in representational thought. The eternal return escapes the trappings of negation through the force of active forgetting. Nietzsche, and therefore also Deleuze, posit forgetfulness against the memory complexes of duration to sidestep the act of negation, which relies upon the identity of essence in its operation. Without memory, there is nothing, or no "thing," to negate. We are left with intensities, and ultimately, singularities that have lost all chains of association, even at the molecular level. To reconnect to Leibniz's calculus, this is the differential equation, where $dy/dx$ forces the terms to infinitely approach 0, always-already vanishing, while the relation itself remains determinable. The differential mechanism is the quasi-cause, and the molar memory of actual forms is expelled through the infinite splitting of the past and future in the self-differing eluded present. Absolute becoming, the function of counter-causality, creates a gap between the future and the past. It makes a ghost of duration and divides the past from the future *in perpetuum,* forcing all three syntheses of time to become according to the logical planes of their operation, whether in sensation or ideational events. An ordinate of the circle, the moment unwinds the circle of the past as a synthesis of the future. This is the portrait of Deleuze's eternal return that is most prevalent in the secondary literature: the broken circle of time stretched out in a straight line. The third synthesis of time, or the future, finds its most exhaustive exposition in *Difference and Repetition.* The future is emptied of content, including all duration; it is the repetition of the unconditioned. By usurping the ground of the pure past, the third synthesis of time expresses the death of God and man, and appropriately, the destruction of all identity. The result is a metaphysical system, Nietzschean to the core, whereby aesthetic ontology replaces the judgment of Reason. Through the use of quasi-causality, the two inverted modes of becoming — sensory becoming and absolute becoming — constitute a world of pre-individual singularities, without negation, binary structures, or any of the trappings of Being. Unity, identity, duration (permanence), substance, cause, and materiality are unhinged from Reason in philosophy. In the end, Deleuze invents a logic of becoming that produces an aesthetic metaphysical system expressive of Nietzsche's Dionysian world.

3

# Closed Vessels and Signs:
## Jealousy as a Passion for Reality

*Arjen Kleinherenbrink*

Gilles Deleuze's *Proust and Signs* is a philosophical investigation of Marcel Proust's *In Search of Lost Time* revolving around the concept of jealousy. According to Deleuze, Proust expands the experience of jealousy into a veritable "logic of jealousy" which discloses that reality is "a schizoid universe of closed vessels."[1] Deleuze explicates this logic by tracing how the Proustian lover's jealousy fuels an apprenticeship in which a beloved is successively experienced in terms of four signs: "material signs" of worldliness, love, and sensuous qualities, and "immaterial signs" of art. At each stage, the lover learns not just something about the beloved, but also about things in general. The signs, however, do not refer to four kinds of entities or experiences. There is only a formal distinction between them, and together they constitute a theory of the experience and essence of any entity whatsoever, be it a love, a memory, a person, a madeleine, or cobblestones.

Reconstructing Deleuze's analysis is interesting for two reasons. First, probing a seemingly banal feeling for philosophical riches far surpassing its specificity as a contingent passion

1   Gilles Deleuze, *Proust and Signs,* trans. Richard Howard (Minneapolis: University of Minnesota Press, 2000), 140, 175.

strongly resonates with the analyses of anxiety, boredom, and nausea in the respective philosophies of Søren Kierkegaard, Martin Heidegger, and Jean-Paul Sartre. Jealousy, however, is not among the usual states investigated by such existentialists and phenomenologists, making it a relatively fresh ground to cover. Second, the "schizoid" universe to which jealousy leads us will be one of individual entities! This is, at the very least, quite surprising from a thinker so often considered to propagate the abolition of individual things in favor of more primordial intensities and fluxes of desire.

*Material signs*

But we must start at the beginning. The lover initially experiences "worldly signs."[2] These are our everyday experiences of things in terms of colors, sounds, sizes, positions, and so on. They are the qualities we usually treat as *being* the objects to which they belong: "the worldly sign does not refer to something, it 'stands for' it, claims to be equivalent to its meaning."[3] After all, we say that madeleines are sweet, cobblestones are heavy, and the beloved is a lover's beloved. These signs characterize the world of habitual recognition, and a non-jealous lover is precisely one who trusts that the beloved is only what she shows him, assuming an identity between her being and his experience of her affections. He believes to truly be part of her world as well, being present to her just as he is. This natural attitude toward things is what Deleuze calls "objectivism": "To refer a sign to the object that emits it, to attribute to the object the benefit of the sign, is first of all the natural direction of perception or of representation."[4] Objectivism, however, is illusory. It makes us believe qualities are out there in the object, rather than *in here* in experience: "we think that the 'object' itself has the

2   Ibid., 6.
3   Ibid.
4   Ibid., 29.

secrets of the signs it emits."[5] Objectivism is false because the same object can sustain contrary qualities. It can be experienced as bright, dull, and ugly now, but as dark, exciting, and beautiful later while nevertheless remaining *this* entity. A friend we have not seen in years may have changed completely, but it remains her. As Deleuze reminds us, the frivolous nature of qualities already moved Plato to dismiss them as merely superficial.[6] The same object can even sustain contrary qualities simultaneously, as being bigger than something is always also being smaller than something else, and being to the left of this is always also being to the right of that.

For Deleuze objectivism is our natural way of looking at things, deeply ingrained in memories, practical activities, perceptions, passions, and thoughts.[7] Hence interrupting our objectivist habits requires a violent shock to thought, which is what jealousy provides. It makes a lover think that an entity (the beloved) is not the qualities in terms of which he experiences it (her). No matter what he experiences her saying or doing, none of it can be trusted, all of it could be lies and deceptions! Poisonous suspicions rear their heads: if she is not how I experience her, then neither am I how she experiences me. So how can *I* be part of her world? And if she does not coincide with the affections she gives me, then others may share her affections as well! Since everything is usually known by its worldly signs, their sudden unreliability makes the jealous lover suspect that he does not really know anything! As Proust writes: "his merciless jealousy places him [...] in the position of a man who does not yet know."[8]

Jealousy then makes the lover encounter "signs of love."[9] These are the same signs as before, but apprehended differently.

5   Ibid., 32.
6   Ibid., 101.
7   Ibid., 27, 29.
8   Marcel Proust, *In Search of Lost Time, Volume I: Swann's Way,* trans. Charles Kenneth Scott Moncrieff and Terence Kilmartin (New York: The Modern Library, 1992), 502–3.
9   Deleuze, *Proust and Signs,* 7.

Qualitative experience is no longer assumed to coincide with its object, but taken as a sign of something hidden within it: "[T]o love is to try to *explicate,* to *develop* these unknown worlds that remain enveloped within the beloved."[10] The lover discovers that things are always in excess over and above the qualities they display: "Names, persons, and things are crammed with a content that fills them to bursting."[11] He realizes he does not love the beloved's superficial qualities, but rather the multiplicity which they translate or transmute: "[L]ove does not concern only […] loved beings, but the multiplicity of souls or worlds in each of them."[12] Readers familiar with Deleuze will immediately recognize this theme. All his works affirm that "*relations are external to terms,*" meaning that the being of an entity (the term) is never directly present in how it is experienced (the relation).[13] In *Difference and Repetition,* the virtual Idea of a problematic being cannot be reduced to its actualization in qualified extension. In *The Logic of Sense,* a body's singularities engender experienced sense-events from which they differ in kind. The body without organs of *Anti-Oedipus* has its desire which animates how it operates as a desiring-machine, but machines experience one another in terms of partial objects and qualified flows according to their capacities, never in terms of desire as such. Despite changes in terminology, Deleuze's recurring thesis is that an entity is neither what it is made of, nor how it is experienced, nor what it does, did, or will do. It is what it can do, so that it is always fundamentally in excess over all its actualizations.

The lover's suspicions are thus confirmed: she is not his. How he experiences her is a real expression of her being, but never this being itself. According to Deleuze, this is the bitter truth of jealousy. The jealous lover keeps longing for full possession of the beloved and for a world in which her affections are purely devoted to him, but at the same time he realizes all too well that

10  Ibid.
11  Ibid., 122.
12  Ibid., 9.
13  Gilles Deleuze and Claire Parnet, *Dialogues,* trans. Hugh Tomlinson and Barbara Habberjam (New York: Columbia University Press, 1987), 55.

this cannot be the case. The beloved always has an excessive world of her own, and at any moment she remains fully capable of dedicating herself to others. Moreover, as the same excessive being applies to all beings, this works both ways: he is excluded from her as she is excluded from him: "the truth of love is first of all the isolation of the sexes."[14] Everything has its own world and one can only experience according to what one can do given one's varying desire, singularities, or *puissance*. All possible experience can only contain translations or caricatures of other entities, never their raw desire, singularities, or excess itself. Therefore whoever interprets love's signs is an interpreter of lies and deceptions, though these terms have no moral connotation here. The point is merely that thinking we can be fully present to the beloved has turned out to be illusory. If love "makes it a principle to renounce all communication" it is because the beloved, by definition, never truly appears to us as such.[15]

The lover, however, does not abide. Jealousy has taken hold of him, with all its relentless suspicions, its betrayals perceived everywhere, and its compulsion to possess and exhaust, to "imprison the beloved, immure her, sequester her in order to 'explicate' her, that is, to empty her of all the worlds she contains."[16] Despite realizing that what he loves in her is her excessive being, the jealous lover can neither tolerate that the beloved cannot be reduced to his relation to her, nor accept that her world may not revolve around him. As Deleuze puts it: "nothing is ever pacified by a *philia*."[17] What will be the jealous lover's next move? He will stubbornly dissect his experience of the beloved in order to isolate those features which characterize her most intimately. Deleuze suggests this is what any subject will attempt after concluding that fleeting qualities cannot be the essence of any object. We can accept that "heavy" and "sweet" are not the essence of cobblestones or madeleines, but our usual response is to look

14  Deleuze, *Proust and Signs*, 80.
15  Ibid., 42.
16  Ibid., 121.
17  Ibid., 122.

for other knowable qualities which would capture the essence anyway. We act as if worldly signs can be separated into two groups, the first consisting of lies and deceptions, the second consisting of truthful signs which communicate the essence of an object to a subject. A Lockean hunt for primary qualities thus ensues. As it is subjects who will have to study their object in order to decide which qualities belong to which group, Deleuze calls this "subjective compensation":

> [W]e are disappointed when the object does not give us the secret we were expecting. [...] How is this disappointment, in each realm, to be remedied? On each line of the apprenticeship, the hero undergoes an analogous experience, at various moments: *for the disappointment of the object, he attempts to find a subjective compensation.* [...] What is to be done except to compensate for the disappointment? To become personally sensitive to less profound signs that are yet more appropriate [...].[18]

Subjective compensation is a tremendous increase in effort, a heroic attempt to know and control the beloved's most profound qualities, to get closer and become more intimate than any possible rival, to strip away all her accidental features in order to unveil what distinguishes her from everything else. As Deleuze keeps repeating throughout *Proust and Signs,* it is the attempt to encircle and isolate the beloved's typical talents and traits, so that the jealous lover can say that only he truly knows and deserves her. One could say the lover becomes a passionate Husserlian, trying to isolate and apprehend the *eidos* or most intimate self-being of an individual.[19]

As an example of subjective compensation, Deleuze reminds his readers of a scene in Proust involving an actress, Berma, who

18  Ibid., 34–35, 36.
19  Edmund Husserl, *Ideas Pertaining to a Pure Phenomenology and to a Phenomenological Philosophy I,* trans. Fred Kersten (Dordrecht: Kluwer, 1982), 7.

through the act of subjective compensation is found to have a strikingly intelligent vocal style. In isolating such a quality, one may think to have found something that truly characterizes her. At last, something "deep" presents itself in experience, something that cannot possibly be a merely superficial and fleeting quality! A jealous lover will try to uncover a set of such qualities, both to prove to himself that he knows the beloved better than anyone else, and to gain data for his plans to isolate her for himself. At first sight, then, it seems he can solve his problem by becoming a master interpreter of signs of love. Whenever "deep" qualities are found, however, it turns out that "the moment of compensation remains in itself inadequate and does not provide a definitive revelation."[20] Despite the lover's efforts, subjective compensation again results in objective disappointment, in a failure to grasp the essence! What has happened? The jealous lover has discovered that something stands between him and the beloved, that there is always something interfering in the relation between a subject and an object. He discovers a third group of signs which will teach him that encircling and isolating the beloved's essence is impossible in principle: "*nothing* can prevent the disappointment."[21]

The third group of signs are what Deleuze calls "sensuous impressions or qualities."[22] Again these are the same signs as before, but again they are apprehended differently. Think of what the jealous lover is doing. He is trying to identify the beloved's most intimate traits, those which deeply resonate with her and that truly make her flourish when "activated." He is constantly imagining or trying to realize situations in which she will truly "shine forth," hoping that if he offers her these situations, she will elect to reside in them, together with him and in all sincerity. Have not all of us at some point fantasized about the ultimate gesture and the perfect collision of interests that would unite us with the beloved once and for all, like Bonny and Clyde united

20 Deleuze, *Proust and Signs*, 36.
21 Ibid., 52–3, 35.
22 Ibid., 11.

in a passion for crime or the Curies united in a passion for science? The jealous lover, however, learns that such situations are sources of defeat instead of victory. Even if he manages to create and sustain them he will not have the beloved's essence, but only her manifestations at a certain place and time! It does not matter that those would be situations in which she is "at home" or "at her best." She will still manifest only as a caricature or transmutation and he will only love her according to circumstances. The very fact that "deep" qualities are only actualized in very specific situations *and* that the jealous lover must fantasize or realize even more circumstances in which to "reactivate" them, teaches him that there is no quality independent of circumstance. There is no such thing as an *eidos* or primary quality belonging just to the object! The jealous lover discovers that "[T]he reasons for loving never inhere in the person loved but refer to ghosts, to Third Parties, to Themes that are incarnated in himself according to complex laws."[23] Or in less poetic terms: "[T]he quality no longer appears as a property of the object that now possesses it, but as the sign of an *altogether different* object that we must try to decipher, at the cost of an effort that always risks failure."[24] The lover finds himself confronted with a necessary consequence of relations being external to terms: there is no universal medium through or ground upon which relations can be forged. If there would be, all relations and terms would be internal to one term: the medium or ground (its historical guises are famous: *Apeiron*, God, Nature, Spirit, and so on). Instead, the ground is always a contingent entity, with the ground as well as what relates on it remaining irreducible to one another. There is no medium, there are "various media."[25] As Deleuze says in an early seminar on the problem of grounding:

> The ground is the third, because it is neither the claimant, nor what he lays claim to, but the instance which will make

23  Ibid., 31.
24  Ibid., 11.
25  Ibid., 49.

the claimed yield to the claimant. The object in itself is never subjected to the claim. The demand and the claim always come to the object from the outside. Example: in making a claim to the hand of the girl, what can one appeal to? As arbiter we use the father who is the third, the ground. But the father can say: complete a test, slay the dragon. What grounds is then the test. [He] can also say that it depends on her. There is then still a third. The love the girl experiences is not like her being itself, but the principle which makes her being yield to the claim. There is always a third and it has to be sought out [...].[26]

Subjective compensation fails. Isolating eidetic qualities and tailoring a situation to them does not yield possession of the beloved. To his horror, the lover realizes that *any* sign or experience is a mere translation of his beloved's fundamental excess over all relation, and also that the experience of his beloved's qualities is irrevocably characterized and colored by the contingent third thing in which experience happens. We are wrong in thinking that we can be subtle or even scientific enough to accurately isolate the essence of an object and bring it into the light of day. Returning to the example of the actress, our hero discovers that her remarkable qualities manifest only in the role of Phèdre that Berma plays.[27] They belong not just to Berma, but to Berma on stage and in character. This is why Deleuze associates Third Parties with involuntary memories "rising up," as with Combray for the madeleine and Venice for the cobblestones: any entity whatsoever can only be experienced as tinged by some medium in which it appears. There is simply no other way. If relations are external to terms, a third thing must bring them together. Even if Combray or Venice would not rise up, the madeleine or the cobblestones would still be experienced in something else. Even after the father's blessing and the dragon's

---

26  Gilles Deleuze, *What is Grounding?*, trans. Arjen Kleinherenbrink (Grand Rapids: &&& Publishing, 2015), 22–23.

27  Deleuze, *Proust and Signs,* 37.

death, the claimant and the girl only have each other according to their love. Any qualitative experience is thus common to two things: a "present" of the object at hand and a "past" of that in which it appears.[28] In *Proust and Signs* Deleuze describes the third thing in terms of "rising up." In *The Logic of Sense,* it is the paradoxical entity which "runs through" any two series. In *Anti-Oedipus,* it is the body without organs which 'falls back onto' production wherever two machinic entities establish a connection. No pure appearance is possible, which is why signs of love "anticipate in some sense their alteration and their annihilation" and "love unceasingly prepares its own disappearance [and] acts out its dissolution."[29]

What keeps the jealous lover from grasping the beloved in her unique essence? The previous three signs are "too material."[30] "Material" does not mean "made of physical stuff," but "in something else": "[A]ll the signs we meet in life are still material signs, and their meaning, because it is always *in something else,* is not altogether spiritual."[31] The three material signs always concern the experience of something in terms of what it is not. This is to say they are *relational.* Worldly signs relate entities to general concepts and generic qualities which can always be the same as or like those of other entities. Signs of love relate the excessive powers or singularities of an entity to their translation into sensible experience: "[they] are inseparable from the weight of a face, from the texture of a skin, from the width and color of a cheek."[32] Finally, sensuous signs are inextricably mixed with the third thing, the ground or circumstance in and according to which an entity is experienced. Nevertheless, even though progressing through the first three signs teaches him a great deal about reality, the jealous lover who keeps failing to grasp the beloved's essence considers them waste of time. In each case, her essence was "no longer master of its own incarnation, of its own

28  Ibid., 59.
29  Ibid., 19.
30  Ibid., 58.
31  Ibid., 41, emphasis added.
32  Ibid., 85.

choice, but [...] chosen according to data that remain external to it."[33]

The jealous lover thus cannot stop "the Search." First, because he loves her and not how she appears. Second, because his jealousy forces him to seek out the truth of her essence, not its translations. He remains haunted by the thought of being an observer who up to now "saw things only from without, that is to say, who saw nothing."[34] His jealousy is a passion for her reality. Even if he acknowledges that all ways of having her and of being had by her are only ever treacherous transmutations, and even if this is true for all lovers and beloveds, he must still find the essence of which these transmutations are translations. In Deleuze's words: "At the end of the Search, the interpreter understands [...] that the material meaning is nothing without an ideal essence that it incarnates. The mistake is to suppose that the hieroglyphs represent 'only material objects.'"[35] The lover will take one last step, going beyond the previous signs and toward her essence. And since jealousy fuels his need to know what it is he loves and wants to possess, "jealousy is deeper than love, it contains love's truth."[36]

*Immaterial signs*

Materiality is operation in or according to something else. If the lover wants to discover what incarnates itself in material signs, he needs to bracket all (his) ways of putting his beloved in relations: "The beloved woman conceals a secret, even if it is known to everyone else. The lover himself conceals the beloved: a powerful jailer."[37] He needs to think her internal reality, her

---

33  Ibid., 64.

34  Proust, *In Search of Lost Time*, 532.

35  Deleuze, *Proust and Signs*, 13. "Hieroglyphs" is a synonym for "signs" throughout the book. "Only material objects" paraphrases "[...] they regarded aesthetic merits as material objects which an unclouded vision could not fail to discern [...]" (Proust, *In Search of Lost Time*, 207).

36  Deleuze, *Proust and Signs*, 9.

37  Ibid., 79.

immaterial essence external to all relation. Deleuze calls immaterial essences "signs of art": "the world of art is the ultimate world of signs, and these signs, as though dematerialized, find their meaning in an ideal essence."[38] Why art? Because art allows us to see that an entity is never what it relates to, neither its component parts nor its observers. The Mona Lisa is not reducible to the paint and canvas from which it emerges (even though it needs both to survive), to how it is experienced, to whom created it, nor to who it depicts. This is the lover's epiphany: the beloved has an essence irreducible to all relation. Art is what can "*stand up on its own*"; it is the exception teaching us the truth for all cases.[39] Yet what is this essence? It is a unity: "[A]rt gives us the true unity: unity of an immaterial sign and of an entirely spiritual meaning. The essence is precisely this unity of sign and meaning as it is revealed in the work of art."[40] What is the bond between this immateriality and spirituality? "It is a difference, the absolute and ultimate Difference. Difference is what constitutes being [...]."[41] This difference is *not* "an empirical difference between two things or two objects, always extrinsic."[42] It does not concern a relation of one entity with another. Instead, it is the intrinsic difference constituting the internal reality of an entity. But what is this internal reality? Deleuze tells us that essence is an "Idea," but also that Proust is Leibnizian in that essences are "veritable monads."[43] These two statements are the key to understanding signs of art, because it indicates that the essence of an entity has two aspects.

The Idea was already encountered earlier: "when we have reached the revelation of art, we learn that essence was already

38  Ibid., 13.
39  Gilles Deleuze and Félix Guattari, *What Is Philosophy?,* trans. Hugh Tomlinson and Graham Burchell (New York: Columbia University Press, 1994), 164.
40  Deleuze, *Proust and Signs,* 40.
41  Ibid., 41.
42  Ibid.
43  Ibid.

there."[44] It is that of which signs of love were translations: the fundamental excess of the being of the beloved. Her Idea is her desire, her *puissance,* her singularities, her virtuality, that which she can do. Since every worldly sign is a sign of love as well, an entity's Idea is always subsisting in how we actually experience it: "the Idea is already there in the sign, in the enveloped and involuted state, in the obscure state of what forces us to think."[45] And if Deleuze famously takes up the Nietzschean challenge to invert Platonism, it is not just by making Ideas interior essences. He also makes Ideas malleable. His is not a Platonic theory in which "the Idea as the goal of reminiscence is the stable Essence," but one in which Ideas are subject to "qualitative transition" and "mutual fusion."[46] Essence is neither fixed nor directly knowable. This is why the entire book puts so much emphasis on learning. Not just because the jealous lover undergoes an apprenticeship, but also because the Idea of an entity can change, depending on its encounters, best exemplified by learning in human beings.

But an essence is not just an Idea. Essence is a unity of an Idea with what Deleuze calls "the hidden thing," "the concealed thing," found to "dwell in dark regions."[47] In terms of his other works: each plastic Idea is wedded to its problem, singularities are always tied to a body in a depth, and wherever there is desire there is a body without organs. This is why essences are *veritable* monads. The Leibnizian monad in itself is a bond between the absolute simple spiritual substance and its real qualities.[48] It is also why essences are "viewpoints."[49] Each entity, after all, can only experience a world based on what its powers enable it to

---

44  Ibid., 89.

45  Ibid., 97.

46  Ibid., 109.

47  Ibid., 47, 100.

48  Each monad must have real qualities, otherwise they would not be distinct. See Gottfried Wilhelm Leibniz, "The Principles of Philosophy, or, The Monadology," in *Philosophical Essays,* trans. and eds. Roger Ariew and Daniel Garber (Cambridge: Hackett Publishing, 1989), §8, 213–24.

49  Deleuze, *Proust and Signs,* 161.

experience and do. Of course this seems strange: is Deleuze not the thinker of free-floating intensities, flows of desire, rhizomes, and a chaos of infinite speeds? The point is nevertheless that while entities are always already enmeshed in complex networks and fluid intersections with countless others, nothing can take away the fact that every entity is irreducible, even though its essence may change over the course of its existence. Deleuze is first and foremost a thinker of individual entities, even if he always thinks them in their becomings. And indeed, a hidden "realm" of permeating intensities or throbbing desire is *not at all* what the jealous lover finds. The lover and the beloved are not just "physically" separated while "really" being together as free flows somewhere else. Because what does the jealous lover find once he has reached the essence? By discovering the essence of the beloved, he discovers any given entity is essentially a sealed or closed vessel, one closed by definition, a point Deleuze keeps repeating.[50] The essence of an entity is thus the tension between its monadic simplicity as a closed vessel and its malleable Idea determining what it can do. This is the meaning of "difference in itself" and "internal difference," because it constitutes absolute heterogeneity within a single entity. As Deleuze insists in *Proust and Signs,* essences are "imprisoned" in a state of "*complication,* which envelops the many in the One and affirms the unity of the multiple."[51] Finally, then, the jealous lover has reached the Real, and "this ideal reality, this virtuality, is essence […]."[52] He at last discovers the root cause of things, an essence irreducible to a psychological state, a transcendental subjectivity, or any de-rivative thereof: "[T]he final quality at the heart of a subject; but this quality is deeper than the subject, of a different order. […] Essence is not only individual, it *individualizes.*"[53] Now, it is easy to see why essence individualizes. The individual beloved and all her individual qualities and actions are mere actualizations of

50  Ibid., 117, 125, 127, 162, 175.
51  Ibid., 45.
52  Ibid., 61.
53  Ibid., 43.

her virtual essence as translated in terms of both circumstance (remember the sensuous signs) and the Idea or capacities of the lover. Any actual experienced individual is always a translated blend of the object perceived and that in which the object is perceived, based on the capacities of the perceiver. At the same time that essence is incarnated in a substance, "the ultimate quality constituting it is therefore expressed as the quality common to two different objects, kneaded in this luminous substance, plunged into this refracting medium."[54] Hence any actual event is grounded in essences, the latter being the veritable causes of all previous signs:

> It is only on the level of art that the essences are revealed. But once they are manifested in the work of art [...], we learn that they already incarnated, that they were *already* there in all these kinds of signs [...].[55]

## Schizoid universe

The jealous lover does not find a solution, but a reason. He learns why it is impossible to truly possess the beloved. The beloved, like each entity, *is* the immaterial unity of a closed vessel wedded to a malleable Idea, only appearing in relation by being translated or transmuted, by being co-constituted by the essences of other entities. Essences can only be thought, never made present: "in the case of the signs of art, pure thought as the faculty of essences becomes the interpreter."[56] Or put differently: "The intelligence dreams of objective content, of explicit objective significations that it is able, of its own accord, to discover or to receive or to communicate."[57] Note that this is not ontotheology. The jealous lover knows that entities are sealed vessels wedded to shifting desire, but precisely because such essences cannot ap-

54  Ibid., 47.
55  Ibid., 38.
56  Ibid., 86.
57  Ibid., 29, cf. "only intelligence extracts truth" (ibid., 23).

pear in relations without being transmuted, he can never know precisely what exists and what something can do. Hence "there is no intersubjectivity except an artistic one,"[58] because every relation will always already be the result of a styling of experience. Deleuze's famous mantra states that we know not what a body can do, and the jealous lover discovers why: "jealousy is [...] the discovery of the unknowable world that represents the beloved's own viewpoint [...]."[59]

The Search culminates in the grand thesis that reality is "a schizoid universe of closed vessels, of cellular regions, where contiguity itself is a distance [...]."[60] Not just for us, but as such. Being is not ontologically split into subjects and objects; rather, *both* of them are equals in being sealed vessels or bodies: "neither things nor minds exist, there are only bodies."[61] The world itself "has become crumbs and chaos."[62] It is a world in which each "part is valid for itself, [and] there is no other part that corresponds to it, no totality into which it can enter, no unity from which it is torn and to which it can be restored."[63]

It follows that entities must be thought as contingent alliances between heterogeneous, irreducible parts, with each part consisting of further such parts, each with a body and desire of its own:

We can form a complex group, but we never form it *without its splitting in its turn, this time as though into a thousand sealed vessels.* [...] [A]nd in each vessel is a self that lives, perceives, desires, and remembers, that wakes or sleeps, that dies, commits suicide, and revives in abrupt jolts.[64]

58  Ibid., 42.
59  Ibid., 139.
60  Ibid., 175.
61  Ibid., 92.
62  Ibid., 111.
63  Ibid., 112.
64  Ibid., 124.

This is why the relation of parts to a whole is never one of exhaustion, totalization, or "natural place," but instead "the co-existence of asymmetric and noncommunicating parts."[65] This is no less the case for the hydrogen and oxygen in water than it is for two lovers in love. Nothing can truly lock anything in place: "Even [a] painting by Vermeer is not valid as a Whole because of the patch of yellow wall planted there as a fragment of still another world."[66] The essence of an entity cannot be reduced to that in which it appears: "a content [is] incommensurable with the container."[67] For example, when drinking tea "the true container is not the cup, but the sensuous quality, the flavor."[68] The content is the tea *qua* tea, and the flavor is the container into which it is translated, the tea being destined to subsist in it without ever appearing as it is itself. An essence is always implicated in how it is explicated, but that which is explicated cannot become the explication itself. In being experienced by another entity, a "sealed vessel" is treated as an "open box," but this never happens without a fundamental distortion.[69]

The jealous lover has thus discovered a "galactic structure" as the truth of jealousy.[70] It turns out that objectivism is not wrong because objects would not exist, but because it misunderstands what objects are: "objectivity can no longer exist except in the work of art, […] solely in the formal structure of the work, in its style," style being "a matter of essence."[71] So wherever there is a whole, it is not a totality which exhausts or naturalizes its parts. Instead, parts are always only "violently stuck together despite their unmatching edges,"[72] whether they are parts of a perception, Venice, a memory of Combray, a Madeleine, the beloved, or even the beloved and the lover as parts of a love. Complete

65  Ibid., 117.
66  Ibid., 114.
67  Ibid., 117.
68  Ibid., 119.
69  Ibid., 140.
70  Ibid., 175.
71  Ibid., 167.
72  Ibid., 123.

totalities do not exist and "this is what the closed vessels signify: there is no totality except a statistical one that lacks any profound meaning."[73] Nothing is ever locked in place, everything in any relation can in principle escape and deterritorialize: there are only "aberrant communications between the noncommunicating vessels, transversal unities between the boxes that resist any totalization […]."[74]

The world thus discovered revolves around "force."[75] Everything, ranging from simple perception, to forging an amorous relation, to keeping one's parts in place, is a matter of struggle between parts that have no natural place, no reason as such to be anywhere as anything. This is the necessary consequence of the "astonishing pluralism" Deleuze finds in Proust.[76] If nothing has a natural place, if nothing can be related to as such, then relating to anything at all requires work, force, effort, translation, deceit, maintenance, strategy, and luck. Moreover, *learning* becomes the highest task:

> To learn is first of all to consider a substance, an object, a being as if it emitted signs to be deciphered, interpreted. There is no apprentice who is not "the Egyptologist" of something. One becomes a carpenter only by becoming sensitive to the signs of wood, a physician by becoming sensitive to the signs of disease. […] Everything that teaches us something emits signs; every act of learning is an interpretation of signs or hieroglyphs.[77]

We can never learn what something is in and of itself. This fails in principle. Instead, we must learn how, where, when, and why something works, which is to become sensitive to the signs something emits. Such is the final meaning of jealousy as the passion proper to the apprenticeship of signs. And just as jeal-

73  Ibid., 125–26.
74  Ibid., 143.
75  Ibid., 152.
76  Ibid., 4.
77  Ibid.

ousy makes the Proustian lover stumble upon an unexpected universe of closed vessels, so could Deleuze's treatment of jealousy introduce us to an unexpected Deleuze, both in terms of where his affinities lie and of what his axioms are.

# 4

# The Drama of *Ressentiment*:
# The Philosopher versus the Priest

*Sjoerd van Tuinen*

Following the terrorist attack on Charlie Hebdo on January 7, 2015, Slavoj Žižek took a stance against the consensus that the assailants were fundamentalists. A true fundamentalist, after all, is deeply convinced of the superiority of his own way of life and therefore indifferent toward the non-believers' way of life. When a Tibetan Buddhist encounters a Western hedonist, he may note that the hedonist's search for happiness is self-defeating, but he will not condemn him for this. Today's pseudo-fundamentalists, by contrast, are deeply bothered, intrigued, fascinated by the sinful life of global consumerism. In fighting the other, they are in fact fighting themselves, and this is what makes them all the more passionate. The terrorists, Žižek argues, are driven not by self-confidence but by *ressentiment*:

> How fragile the belief of a Muslim must be if he feels threatened by a stupid caricature in a weekly satirical newspaper? […] The problem with fundamentalists is not that we consider them inferior to us, but, rather, that *they themselves* secretly consider themselves inferior. This is why our condescending politically correct assurances that we feel no superiority towards them only makes them more furious and feeds their resentment. The problem is not cultural difference (their ef-

fort to preserve their identity), but the opposite fact that the fundamentalists are already like us, that, secretly, they have already internalized our standards and measure themselves by them.[1]

*Ressentiment,* according to Friedrich Nietzsche, is the feeling of vengefulness.[2] According to Gilles Deleuze's succinct definition, it is a reaction which "*ceases to be acted in order to become something felt (senti).*"[3] It results from one's impotence to either change or forget the cause of one's suffering. As interiorized suffering, it turns outward only in the form of moral indignation. For a long time, it was thought that the *ressentimental* need for recrimination and compensation was the main drive behind the French Revolution and subsequent emancipatory processes. Eventually these processes would have led, despite their secret inauthentic motivation as it were, to a mature, i.e., post-historical, post-ideological, and post-political democracy in which all soil on which *ressentiment* grows has been erased. Except that, the rise of populism, fundamentalism, anti-intellectualism, scapegoating, and the whole culture of naming, blaming, shaming, and claiming by people who experience themselves as victims despite living in affluent societies have put the question of *ressentiment* back on the agenda.

1   Slavoj Žižek, "Slavoj Žižek on the Charlie Hebdo massacre: Are the worst really full of passionate intensity?," *New Statesman,* January 10, 2015, http://www.newstatesman.com/world-affairs/2015/01/slavoj-i-ek-charlie-hebdo-massacre-are-worst-really-full-passionate-intensity. In this article, Žižek writes "resentment" but means *ressentiment.* Adam Smith defined resentment as a social passion of injustice. *Ressentiment,* by contrast, equals a degenerated and inauthentic resentment. See Sjoerd van Tuinen, ed., *The Polemics of Ressentiment* (London/New York: Bloomsbury, forthcoming 2017).
2   Friedrich Nietzsche, *On the Genealogy of Morals,* ed. Walter Kaufmann, trans. Walter Kaufmann and Reginald J. Hollingdale, published together with *Ecce Homo,* ed. and trans. Walter Kaufmann (New York: Vintage Books, 1989), 37.
3   Gilles Deleuze, *Nietzsche and Philosophy,* trans. Hugh Tomlinson (New York: Columbia University Press, 2006), 111. My emphasis.

If in the current post-emancipatory condition everybody can see again the actuality of the notion of *ressentiment*, it is not up to philosophy to prove its relevance or sum up the different forms in which it appears. On the contrary: the problem is that our understanding of the various forms of *ressentiment* is hardly ever based on more than some trivial everyday psychology. Liberal conservative discourse is symptomatic in this respect, as it suffices to reduce any emancipatory movement — from Jacobinism to feminism and populism — to its base motivation in jealousy, frustration, or some other passion deemed pathological and/or irrational in order to disqualify it. Of course, this discourse is not exactly new. Just as Nietzsche despised socialism or anarchism as secularizations of a Judaic-Christian *ressentiment* (and in this way dismissed the French Revolution as "a pathetic and bloody *piece of quackery*"[4]), later philosophical sociologists and anthropologists from Max Weber and Max Scheler to René Girard see modern egalitarian struggles as expressions of a dangerously regressive envy. Žižek rightfully wonders whether this "obsessive-compulsive urge to find beneath solidarity the envy of the weak and thirst for revenge [...] is sustained by a disavowed envy and resentment of its own, the envy of the universal emancipatory position."[5] But is his own position really different? Does he not also frame the situation around Charlie Hebdo from a majoritarian point of view, such that the scary and attention seeking "other" turns out to be actually very much like us, only less authentic and more deprived?[6] And in this way, does

4    Friedrich Nietzsche, *Daybreak: Thoughts on the Prejudices of Morality*, eds. Maudemarie Clark and Brian Leiter, trans. Reginald J. Hollingdale (Cambridge: Cambridge University Press, 1997), 211.
5    Slavoj Žižek, *Violence: Six Sideways Reflections* (London: Profile Books, 2009), 287.
6    Wendy Brown, for example, has made the classical argument that in the multiculturalist mantra of race, class, gender, sexuality, *ressentiment* invariably names class difference but rarely articulates it as such. Thus while she agrees with Žižek that identity politics and its discourse of injustices other than class covers up the subject's investment in the internal standards of existing societies, such that no difference is counted as a real difference, her analysis has the merit of taking this argument out of the

he not reinforce the very opposition his diagnosis is supposed to overcome?[7]

In fact, the problem of *ressentiment* is much more obstinate than is generally acknowledged. In his *On the Genealogy of Morals,* Nietzsche himself was very explicit about the fact that for him *ressentiment* was not a psychological (or historical, or even biological) problem, but first of all a philosophical problem, the problem of a philosophical clinic.[8] This explains why in his work, the critical unmasking of *ressentiment* rarely takes the form of a personal reproach or of the attempt to outsmart his opponents by psychopathological means. Whereas Nietzsche would undoubtedly agree with Žižek that such recriminating uses of the notion bespeak a *ressentimental* moralism of their own, part of the problem is precisely how to prevent this diagnosis from regressing into a never-ending blame game. Following Deleuze's leading thesis in *Nietzsche and Philosophy,* everything happens as if Nietzsche has not been taken seriously enough as a philosopher (i.e., as a "pedagogue of the concept"). Warning us like no other of the "modern conformism" in our use of Nietzsche, Deleuze conveys a very "demoralizing" message: it is crucial to emphasize the radically "extra-moral" character of the concept of *ressentiment*, since this is precisely what has been compromised and betrayed right after Nietzsche. Whereas we can easily speak the truth that belongs to phenomena of *ressentiment*, the practical meaning and affective direction of this truth (its *sens*) is usually not as critical as we think it is. As Deleuze, always wary of the puerility and artificiality of truth judgments, writes: "We always have as much truth as we deserve in accordance with the

blame structure of a liberal order that alternately denies the real grounds of *ressentiment* or blames those who suffer from it for their own condition. Cf. Wendy Brown, "Wounded Attachments," *Political Theory* 31, no. 3 (1993): 390–410.

7   Sjoerd van Tuinen, "A Thymotic Left?: Peter Sloterdijk and the psychopolitics of *Ressentiment*," *Symploke* 18, nos. 1–2 (2010): 47–64, at 61.

8   Nietzsche, *Genealogy of Morals,* 55–56.

sense of what we say. Sense is the genesis or the production of the true, and truth is only the empirical result of sense."[9]

*Ressentiment*, then, is one of those thorny issues that constantly threaten to compromise the one who speaks about it. There is no intrinsic good sense in the application of its concept and no universal criterion, but only, as we will see, a polemical sense. It is precisely its conflictual politics that is forgotten when, for example, leftist intellectuals blame rightwing populists for pursuing a vulgar politics of rancor, or when the latter blame the traditional leftist elite for being stuck in the past. In fact, the more we tend to think we have overcome our *ressentiment*, the more we should wonder whether our own discursive position is not itself infected by the very moralizing *ressentiment* which we like to think we have acquired the right to dismiss. In what follows, I will practice Deleuze's method of dramatization in order to distinguish two almost opposed senses in which the concept of *ressentiment* has been put to use: a speculative sense and a nihilistic sense. Whereas the former is typical for the conceptual persona of the philosopher, the latter corresponds to that of the priest. I will argue that while there is no a priori rule and no final argument that can mediate or solve their conflict, the former acquires the highest or best consistency between theory and practice in the concept of *ressentiment*.

## *The forgetting of the priest*

Nietzsche proposed the concept of *ressentiment* in order to trace the origins of Western nihilism. While the "morality of morals [*Sittlichkeit der Sitte*]" is constituted in principle, although hardly ever in fact, by the spontaneous activity and creativity of nobles, *ressentiment* is only the local and surreptitious illness of slaves. If this typological difference between aristocrats and slaves is first of all a hierarchy in principle, then because in history it tends to be blurred, distorted or even reversed by *ressenti-*

9   Gilles Deleuze, *Difference and Repetition,* trans. Paul Patton (New York: Columbia University Press, 1994), 154.

*ment*, which fictionalizes a reversal of values in which weakness turns into merit, baseness into humility, passivity into patience, or more generally good into Evil and bad into Good.

How does *ressentiment* become capable of this historical reversal, given the slaves' essential impotence to act? This is the genealogical question par excellence and Nietzsche's answer is extremely original: the victory of reactive forces over active forces is due to the calculating genius of a third type, the (Pauline) priest. The role of the priest is that of a healer or redeemer who suffers from, and relies on, the same illness he is supposed to heal. By a constant appeal to bad conscience, he turns the outward recriminations inward and thus pacifies *ressentiment*, whereas a constant appeal to pity enables him to seduce and reduce even the most noble forces to passivity and thus disseminate *ressentiment* ad infinitum. In protecting the weak against the strong, the priest thus leads the "slave revolt in morality," that moment when "*ressentiment* itself becomes creative and gives birth to values,"[10] in other words, when it constitutes a global culture of its own. From the genealogical point of view the priest is the most important type, because without him it is not clear why the whole of life would succumb to passivity. While *ressentiment* is the source of slave morality, it takes an artist capable of giving an adaptive and regulative form to passive matter for the fictional reversal of values to bring about real effects.[11] It is thus up to the priest to usher in the long history of a postponed and imaginary revenge, even if this revenge will ultimately acquire a secular form in the modern ideal of universal equality, just as the place of the priest will be taken up by demagogues, politicians, journalists, psychotherapists, and all the more anonymous media of contemporary biopolitics.

Authors such as Scheler and Girard also see an intrinsic relation between *ressentiment* and modernity, but following in the

10  Nietzsche, *Genealogy of Morals,* 36.
11  Friedrich Nietzsche, *The Anti-Christ,* published together with *Ecce Homo, Twilight of the Idols,* eds. Aaron Ridley and Judith Norman, trans. Judith Norman (Cambridge: Cambridge University Press, 2005), 21–22; Deleuze, *Nietzsche and Philosophy,* 125–26.

footsteps of Max Weber's criticism of Nietzsche, they reverse the causal relation. Whereas vengefulness would be of all times, they argue, *ressentiment* could only become a formative power because of egalitarian ideals that constantly confront us with a discrepancy between principle and fact, and thus encourage rancor as a universal human right. Whereas the "untimely" originality of Nietzsche's genealogical method lies in emphasizing the necessity of millennia of slow cultural preparation and consolidation, Scheler and Girard turn Nietzsche's genealogical tracing of democratic ideals to *ressentiment* into a much more immediate and determinate, yet also much more trivial and circumstantial connection: only in modern democracies and its egalitarian cultivation of the frustration of the unprivileged over the persistence of inequality could *ressentiment* have its disruptive and militant effect on social order. Instead of the progenitor of modernity, the culture of *ressentiment* would thus be its child. It is no longer *ressentiment* that fictionalizes egalitarian ideology, but egalitarian ideology (what Žižek calls "our standards") that generates *ressentiment*.[12]

Unsurprisingly, it is this inverted perspective that lies at the basis of most modern understandings of *ressentiment*, in which Nietzsche features less as philosophical authority than as half-madman, half-malevolent genius.[13] But the price for this new-found realism is a blindness to the problem that necessitated Nietzsche to invent the concept of *ressentiment* in the first place, i.e., the slave revolt in morality, in which the priest plays a crucial role. We either openly deny (Weber, Scheler, Girard, Charles Taylor) or at least ignore (John Rawls, Ronald Dworkin, Marc Angenot, Marc Ferro, Norbert Bolz) the priestly nature of every culture of *ressentiment*. Instead, we get a retroactive revaluation

12  Max Scheler, *Ressentiment*, trans. William W. Holdheim (New York: Schocken Books, 1972); René Girard, *Deceit, Desire and the Novel: Self and Other in Literary Structure*, trans. Yvonne Freccero (Baltimore: John Hopkins University Press, 1976).

13  Nicholas Birns, "*Ressentiment* and Counter-*Ressentiment*: Nietzsche, Scheler, and the Reaction Against Equality," *Nietzsche Circle*, http://www.nietzschecircle.com/RessentimentMaster.pdf.

of the mediating role of Christianity modelled on, and often also put forward as a model for, civil society.[14] The Christian love of one's neighbor does not turn *ressentiment* into a formative power, but precisely prevents it from becoming so. After all, in Christ we are all equal. Only in modernity is the patient waiting for the Last Judgment transformed into the impatience of the Last Man who wants to be compensated for every suffering and every perceived injustice here on earth. Only here does *ressentiment* become something that can no longer be repressed.

From a Nietzschean point of view, the later confusion of the causality of *ressentiment* with its ideological consequences and the subsequent forgetting of the priest can usually be recognized by two methodological consequences. Firstly, it implies the depoliticization of the concept of *ressentiment* by empirical psychology and neurosciences, which focus on emotions of individuals instead of socio-political passions. Secondly, this depoliticization of *ressentiment* comes at the price of its subsequent sociological moralization, according to which the *ressentiment* of individuals threatens the public order instead of being an intrinsic part of it. But aren't psychologization and moralization precisely the *modus operandi* of the priest as identified by Nietzsche? Is this not exactly how the neo-liberal pacification of the loser as guilty individual, the discrete management of depressed egos, proceeds, arguing that if you were not successful on the market, you have nobody to blame but yourself?[15]

14 The exception here is Žižek, for whom the *ressentiment* of Holocaust victims (rather than that of the Charlie Hebdo attackers) appears to be affirmable as the very persistence of the negative (i.e., as a contradictory "authentic *ressentiment*," see Žižek, *Violence*, 159) instead of having to be negated itself.

15 For a historical development, see Sjoerd van Tuinen, "Physiology versus Psychology: The Priest and the Biopolitics of *Ressentiment*," in *Inside. Outside. Other. The Body in the Work of Gilles Deleuze and Michel Foucault,* eds. Ann-Cathrin Drews and Katharina D. Martin (Bielefeld: Transcript Verlag, forthcoming 2016). Drawing on a distinction from *What Is Philosophy?*, the priest and the philosopher are both psychosocial types and conceptual personae. Psychosocial types are historical constellations. They are defined by what they render perceptible, the three movements

We should remember that the *Genealogy of Morals* is a polemic with priestly modes of thought, and that it opens not simply by rejecting previous attempts to locate the source of Western morality in *ressentiment* made by Paul Rée or Eugen Dühring, but by displacing their inquiry to these moral theorists themselves.[16] It is their rancor, mistrust, impotence, disappointments, ideals, habits, hatred, and tastes, in other words, the typical symptomatology of their will to power, that Nietzsche is interested in. By itself, as a mere historical fact, the problem of *ressentiment* is not interesting. It becomes so only "on the soil of this *essentially dangerous form* of human existence, the priestly form."[17] The relevance of an inquiry into *ressentiment* lies exclusively in the non-trivial struggle against the priests who derive their power from its cultivation, and as we should now add, its interpretation and evaluation. This leads us to a fourth type, the one with which Nietzsche identifies himself: the philosopher, or the true genealogist. For Nietzsche, the meaning we attribute to *ressentiment* constitutes the very conflict that separates the philosopher and the priest as radically incommensurable perspectives of evaluation. Who has the right to wield the concept of *ressentiment* and on the basis of which principle?

of the formation of territories, vectors of deterritorialization and the process of reterritorialization relative to a social field (Gilles Deleuze and Félix Guattari, *What Is Philosophy?,* trans. Hugh Tomlinson and Graham Burchell [New York: Columbia University Press, 1994], 68). Different from psychosocial types, this chapter deals with conceptual personae. These are not physical or mental territories and movements of deterritorialization, but properly spiritual or transcendental conditions of enunciation. They are not relative movements, but problematic powers or affinities that are absolute, belonging only to the element of thought. "These are no longer empirical, psychological, and social determinations, still less abstractions, but intercessors, crystals, or seeds of thought" (ibid., 69). Even if conceptual personae belong by right to thought and only to thought, they are inseparable from psychosocial types that belong to a historical milieu and render perceptible the drama of de- and re-territorialization of a concept. The two constantly refer to each other and combine without ever merging (ibid., 70).

16  Nietzsche, *Genealogy of Morals,* 24–25.
17  Ibid., 33.

## *Transcendental typology*

Every genealogical discussion requires a certain agonal, dramatic or perspectivist sensibility: not for the relativity of truth, but for the truth of the relational, which takes into account the affects of the one who uses the concept of *ressentiment* no less than those of the one to whom it is applied. As Peter Sloterdijk puts it in his essay on cultural struggle (*Kulturkampf*), *Die Verachtung der Massen*:

> Nietzsche's theorem of *ressentiment* as flight of the weak into moralizing contempt for the strong [...] until today has remained the most powerful instrument for the interpretation of the social-psychological relations in mass culture — an instrument of which it is admittedly not easy to say, who could or should wield it. It offers the most plausible description of the behavior of the majorities in modern societies, but also its most polemogenous interpretation — polemogenous, since it reduces the psychic dispositions of individuals who attest themselves morally first-rate motives to reactive and detractive mechanisms of antiverticality on the level of their intimate drives — such that between "truth" and "plausibility" a relation of mutual exclusion sets in. It is plausible nonetheless, as it attests to the quasi-omnipresent need for degradation of humiliated self-consciousness which empirically speaking effectively belongs to it.[18]

Plausibility is disconnected from truth, as Nietzsche already knew, whenever truth becomes a moral, i.e., universalizable or absolute aim in itself. For truth itself then becomes marked by the *ressentiment* of the slave who denies the irreducible "differend" between higher and lower points of view. "[D]ifference,"

18  Peter Sloterdijk, *Die Verachtung der Massen: Versuch über Kulturkämpfe in der modernen Gesellschaft* (Frankfurt am Main: Suhrkamp Verlag, 2000), 56.

Nietzsche writes, "engenders hatred."[19] As a consequence, the plausibility of the diagnosis of *ressentiment*, the real efficacy of the perspectival truth of *ressentiment*, must be proven in another way than merely in the form of a claim to empirical knowledge. It does not suffice to know the difference in point of view; what is crucial is that it is actually and continuously being made by the genealogist himself. Genealogy, as Deleuze emphasizes, means both the origin of value and the value of the origin.[20] Or as Sloterdijk puts it: every attempt to "make a difference" and resist *ressentiment* implies a cultural struggle over the legitimacy and origin of differences in general.[21]

The problem of genealogy, then, is the necessity of distinguishing between high and low, active and *ressentimental* applications of the concept of *ressentiment*, independent from established values and empirical distributions between rich and poor, capitalist and proletarian, elite and mass, man and woman, and so on. "We cannot use the state of a system of forces as it in fact is, or the result of the struggle between forces, in order to decide which are active and which are reactive."[22] High and low are not just empirical values but refer to a difference in the conditions with which their evaluation takes place. After all, if difference is at the origin, the origin itself already includes the inverted image of its own genealogy[23] — for example, the caricaturized form of evolution, whether dialectical (German) or utilitarian (English), or indeed the modernist discourse around *ressentiment*. This is why, even where we are dealing with a single fact such as *ressentiment*, the philosopher and the priest do not interpret and evaluate it in the same way. Rather, they each perceive the ver-

---

19  Friedrich Nietzsche, *Beyond Good and Evil: Prelude to a Philosophy of the Future,* trans. Walter Kaufmann (New York: Vintage Books, 1966), 213n17.

20  "The difference in the origin does not appear at the origin — except perhaps to a particularly practiced eye, the eye which sees from afar, the eye of the far-sighted, the eye of the genealogist" (Deleuze, *Nietzsche and Philosophy,* 5).

21  Sloterdijk, *Die Verachtung der Massen,* 95, 84.

22  Deleuze, *Nietzsche and Philosophy,* 58.

23  Ibid., 56.

sion of *ressentiment* that corresponds to their point of view. The difference between the philosopher and the priest, as Nietzsche announces already in the preface to the *Genealogy of Morals,* is therefore transcendental or "a priori."[24] It is a critical difference, a difference of imagination that is hard to discern within the fact of *ressentiment,* since it is also constitutive of this fact. Or better still: it is made in the fact itself, such that, strictly speaking, we do not even speak of the same fact at all. "To have *ressentiment* or not to have *ressentiment* — there is no greater difference, beyond psychology, beyond history, beyond metaphysics. It is the true difference or transcendental typology — the genealogical and hierarchical difference."[25] The difference can only be discovered when we dramatize the fact of *ressentiment* and effectively construct its concept as a multiplicity of becomings, or put differently, when instead of asking what it is, we ask who it is that claims its truth and what passions are involved.

This is why Deleuze emphasizes Nietzsche's typological approach, which aims to characterize in each thing and in each passion a principle of internal genesis and qualitative difference. Passions are always mixtures of high and low tendencies, such that the noble is constantly translated and reduced by the servile, and the servile is continuously reversed and transmuted by the noble. But whatever the factual mixtures, the fact that the two types do not communicate in the same way effectively proves that they continue to differ in principle. They are different vectors of feeling: while the slave is one of negation, the noble is one of affirmation.[26] If, in addition to the noble and the slave,

24  Nietzsche, *Genealogy of Morals,* Preface 16, 20.
25  Deleuze, *Nietzsche and Philosophy,* 33.
26  Types are neither empirical portraits to be compared against an original, nor ideal types in the Weberian sense. Rather, they are ensembles of forces, which are physiological, but also psychological, political, historical, and social. Deleuze therefore insists that we make a difference between the type of the will to power (quality) and the relations of force (quantity), the former being the sufficient reason for the latter and as such inseparable from, but by no means identical with them (Deleuze, *Nietzsche and Philosophy,* 44). Between them there is no simple opposition (this already betrays the one-sided perspective of negation of difference), but rather a

we also need to distinguish the type of the philosopher and the priest, this is because only the philosopher has an interest in the art of typology. The very artificiality or imaginary character of the types is precisely what enables him to distinguish the deep distances between the grounds on which the passions become empirically visible and truths are produced. And it is this original and originary contrast that must be restored every time the passions are interpreted and evaluated — it is the very condition of their philosophical enunciation. Only on the basis of the distinct type can we diagnose the sense of a mixture: when does *ressentiment* become a problem (at the beginning of history or at its end), in what form does it come about (frustrated revenge or envy), and in what order (as consequence or as principle of justice)?

*Right and fact*

Following Nietzsche and Deleuze, the delicate but rigorous art of the philosopher is to diagnose and evaluate our present becomings by differentiating between high and low, noble or base, and to keep them apart "to all eternity [*für alle Ewigkeit*]."[27] To diagnose is therefore not just to produce an empirical truth about an actual state of affairs, but also, as in medical diagnosis, to propose a strategy of healing and self-overcoming — in other words, to construct a type or symptomatology and negotiate a new vital relation to it. Inseparable from the becomings that insist in the diagnosed, the diagnosis must itself have the power of a performative: "The *diagnosis* of becomings in every passing present is what Nietzsche assigned to the philosopher as physician, 'physician of civilization,' or inventor of new immanent modes of existence."[28] In this sense, philosophers such as

contrast: "two things can be thought as being really distinct without being separable, no matter how little they may have requisites in common" (Gilles Deleuze, *The Fold: Leibniz and the Baroque*, trans. Tom Conley [Minneapolis: University of Minnesota Press], 55).

27  Nietzsche, *Genealogy of Morals*, 138.

28  Deleuze and Guattari, *What Is Philosophy?*, 113.

Baruch Spinoza or Epictetus are interested in the becoming better or active of empirically given affections and passions. Since becoming is not only polar (active or passive) but also complex (a becoming-active of reactive forces or a becoming-reactive of active forces), they would never demand from those to whom the diagnosis applies that they give up or repress their specific passions. For it is these passions which, no matter how negative or sickening, enable the latter to become. An immanent diagnosis must therefore always be both affirmative and speculative. It cannot be content to remain at the level of critical judgment, but has to effectively encounter them in a kind of mutual inclusion or co-presence. It must risk an inventive perspective that renders visible our actual passions at the same time as those virtual passions that can be associated with their becoming. This is how Nietzsche, in *Ecce Homo,* discusses the art of perspectival reversal by which we not only learn to evaluate healthy modes of living from the perspective of the sick, but also to distance ourselves from our illnesses from the fuller perspective of the healthy.[29] The point is that between the two points of view, there is no reciprocity or commensurability, or indeed no pity. A true change of perspectives is already a becoming, a construction of force relations according to a vital mode of evaluation. While the schizophrenic movement from health to illness or from illness to health appears to be double, in reality it is a single movement, a single act of thought. As such it is itself the sign of a virtual health superior to every actual affective state (Nietzsche's "great health").[30] Health, after all, is never a static state, but always also a dynamic act of counter-effectuation: a *Genesung,* both healing and genesis.

With respect to *ressentiment,* too, this means that its overcoming implies a pure becoming, or in other words, a difference that is actively made with respect to every status quo. It is never

29  Friedrich Nietzsche, *Ecce Homo,* published together with *Genealogy of Morals,* 222–23.

30  Gilles Deleuze, *Pure Immanence: Essays on A Life,* trans. Anne Boyman (Brooklyn: Zone Books, 2005), 58.

sufficient to merely establish the individual fact of *ressentiment*. Like every passion, it possesses a "grey zone" where it becomes indiscernible from a whole spectrum of contrasting individuations. *Ressentiment*, as Bernard Stiegler writes, "is the nihilistic face of a combat that must be led within becoming, with it, but in order to transform it into a future." Every becoming is at least duplicitous, such that the worst lies within the best and conversely. "The larger question is, therefore: what must actually be combated, that is, what must one do, after one recognizes the scourge of *ressentiment*?"[31] The diagnosis itself must be dramatized in the virtual presence of a superior tenor of life, such that *ressentiment* becomes that which we cease to embody, not that in which we are locked up. After all, it is never the lower class or the poor who have *ressentiment*, but the slaves, that is, those lacking the potential of becoming. *Ressentiment* is without a doubt bad, but it is not Evil and this means that, instead of judging over it, we need to expose its contagious effects in such a manner that we give it the opportunity to morph into something else. As Deleuze and Guattari put it in *What Is Philosophy?*: "A mode of existence is good or bad, noble or vulgar, complete or empty, independently of Good and Evil or any transcendent value: there are never any criteria other than the tenor of existence, the intensification of life."[32] Only the generous affirmation of this dramatic occasion that is the neutral event of *ressentiment* enables us to distinguish between true and false physicians of civilization, or indeed between the philosopher and the priest. The point is not that the physician must himself be free of *ressentiment*, but rather that he must re-activate or repeat the difference between the noble and servile becomings that insist in *ressentiment* and return them to the level of a drama of thought where one is the intermediary of the other.[33] This hierarchy is precisely

31  Bernard Stiegler, *The Decadence of Industrial Democracies: Disbelief and Discredit,* Volume 1, trans. Daniel Ross and Suzanne Arnold, (Cambridge/ Malden: Polity Press, 2011), 55.
32  Deleuze and Guattari, *What Is Philosophy?*, 74.
33  This is why Deleuze contrasts the theater of repetition with the theater of representation (Deleuze, *Difference and Repetition,* 10).

the genealogical difference that eternally returns in whatever exists at a certain moment and never ceases to select the noble from the *ressentimental* — its eternal return is the very test of their becoming, the only hammer with which the philosopher can crush the "re-" of *ressentiment* and reintegrate the feeling with the wider activity of the world in a becoming-active.

The priest, by contrast, is unable to repeat the original genealogical difference and possesses only a representation of it. As a consequence, he must derive the sense of *ressentiment* from its empirical appearance. For Scheler, for example, *ressentiment* is the lived state of Jews, dwarves, cripples, women, and social democrats, who are forced to repress their envy and frustration by the socio-political order of Wilhelmine Germany. Even if he is factually correct, the real interest of this diagnosis lies in his defense of the values of a heroic-Christian class society.[34] His diagnosis, in other words, produces no new difference and merely identifies and consolidates already differentiated facts. Half a century later, Girard makes an empirically different but formally similar point. Consumer societies set free an unbridled cultivation of envy and ambition, and thus generate a constant experience of lack and insatiability. The only way to curb this explosion of *ressentiment* is to repress or forbid our desires by the transcendent mediation of the Law modeled on the Decalogue ("thou shalt not covet your neighbor's wife" etcetera).[35] Again, we find an exclusively negative representation of our *ressentiment* with no active differentiation between noble and base becomings. Worse still, the egalitarian conception of desire rules out the very possibility of such a difference ("admit it, in the end we all want the same anyway").[36]

34  Max Scheler, *Ressentiment*, trans. William W. Holdheim (New York: The Free Press, 1961), 96, 133, 177. See also Birns, "*Ressentiment* and Counter-*Ressentiment*."

35  René Girard, *I See Satan Fall Like Lightning,* trans. James G. Williams (New York: Orbis Books, 2001).

36  For a more extensive critique of the positions of Scheler and Girard, see Sjoerd van Tuinen, "Links of rechts *ressentiment*? Pedagogie van een concept," *Krisis* 1 (2013): 60–71.

From a genealogical perspective, then, the priest's diagnosis of *ressentiment* is neither plausible nor interesting, precisely because its truth obliterates the difference in the origin and prevents it from changing the facts.[37] In his hands, *ressentiment* is reduced to a conceptual readymade. Like the positivist historian, he is the passive inheritor of forms from the past, but remains blind to the real forces that produced this form and that will continue to develop it in the future. Content with having identified the truth of *ressentiment*'s existence, his hybris is to betray the consistency of its becomings by replacing it with his own law of its mediation and repression. Incapable of seeing difference at the origin, the priest does not believe in any positive future for *ressentiment* but merely invests in the perpetuation of the actual fact as legitimation of his own image of justice.[38] Lacking all sense of cultural elevation, however, this can only be a reverse image, the least imaginative or speculative one. Thus even when the priest is correct to debunk the idea of social or political justice — and as a consequence the cause of political desire and struggle in general — as the ideological mask for the secret revenge of "those who came off badly [*die Schlechthinweggekommenen*]," as Dühring thought, he still sees it topsy-turvy, on the basis of a reactive interpretation of the facts.[39] For such a reduction is too "English," as Nietzsche would say, that is, too utilitarian. It relies entirely on established values and existing categories of recognition and stays methodologically blind for

---

37  Christoph Narholz makes a similar point on (lack of) "interest" as transcendental criterion with respect to Weber's reading of Nietzsche and *ressentiment* in his essays on the sociology of religion. See Christop Narholz, *Die Politik des Schönen* (Berlin: Suhrkamp Verlag, 2012), 22.

38  Tyranny and tragedy, according to Stiegler, are the two forms in which consistence is reduced to existence. (Bernard Stiegler, *Uncontrollable Societies of Disaffected Individuals: Disbelief and Discredit,* Volume 2, trans. Daniel Ross [Cambridge/Malden: Polite Press, 2013], 35). Following Deleuze (and Gilbert Simondon), Stiegler understands the plane of consistency as the schematism of the transcendental imagination, producing an image of a real drama that remains unrepresentable and without analogy yet accompanies every actualization in the imagination (ibid., 77).

39  Deleuze, *Nietzsche and Philosophy,* 73–75.

the difference in principle between high and low, which is now reduced to a historical difference between principle and fact.[40] As a consequence, the priest fails to acquire the diagnostician's "right" to wield the concept of *ressentiment* at the same time that he exhausts its critical power of problematization in "shameful compromises"[41] with the present and reduces those to whom it applies into guilty subsistence.

For the presence of *ressentiment* to be made interesting again for thought, we must re-dramatize its genealogical difference and thus turn it into a singularity that bears within itself the possibility of its transformation. Dramatization is the art of differences that matter, a matter of conceiving of difference differentially. An active genealogy speculates on the plasticity of those it addresses under the guidance of the eternal return's authority of the best.[42] Nietzsche himself sets the example with his concept of bad conscience, which he puts forward in relation to a new conceptual persona, the priest, and in relation to a new image of thought based on the will to power understood from the point of nihilism, the will to truth.[43] Instead of declaring man guilty of being as ignoble to have interpreted his own suffering as a desirable penal state, he says that it is here that man becomes interesting, "more questionable, *worthier* of asking questions; perhaps also worthier — of living?"[44] In this way, he affirms his own distance to the perspective of the priest at the same time that he reclaims the concept of *ressentiment*. Everything happens as the philosopher enters into an athletic competition where what is at stake is who can see furthest, who can stretch his perspective to comprehend not just more facts but also other perspectives, until finally, the other is no longer rejected, but affirmed as the

40  Nietzsche, *Geneaology of Morals,* 17–18.
41  Deleuze and Guattari, *What Is Philosophy?,* 108.
42  For Stiegler, the tragic or dialectic spirit, like the priest, sees *ressentiment* as a fault (*faute*), whereas it is only a flaw (*défaut*) or imperfection (the best as relativization and dynamization of perfection) (Stiegler, *The Decadence of Industrial Democracies,* 55, 58).
43  Deleuze, *What Is Philosophy?,* 83.
44  Nietzsche, *Genealogy of Morals,* 113.

other within the self. It is precisely through his struggle with the priest that the philosopher disentangles *ressentiment* from its internalization in guilt and conceives of it as a mere imperfection under the horizon of the self-overcoming of man. If, as Deleuze argues, the inherited passion of the modern philosopher is shame, "the shame of being human," then in the case of *ressentiment* we should say that the philosopher's shame over the priest's lack of shame constitutes the "pathos of distance" that entitles him to discover in man the project of a future.[45]

## Conceptual personae

The purpose of our dramatization has been to learn to differentiate, with Nietzsche, between philosophical and priestly manners of diagnosing *ressentiment*. The two types function as markers or references whenever the sense of the concept of *ressentiment* is to be determined. Everything happens as if the concept, even before it was first created, was already internally divided between different, asymmetrical modes in which it can be thought and exercised. The actual concept is signed Nietzsche, but the problem it answers to retains a pre-individual and impersonal problematic, a multiplicity of unknown movements of thought that insist one in the other. This is why Deleuze and Guattari emphasize that Nietzsche's concept of *ressentiment* is inseparable from the various conceptual personae that form its "intercessors," its real thinking subjects of enunciation or "thought-events" by which the concepts come alive and become oriented.[46] Conceptual personae are the powers of imagination that function as navigators and compass in the determination of the undetermined concept. For if the will to power together with the eternal return of difference is Nietzsche's plane of immanence (and the critique of the will to truth is his image of

---

45 On shame as the inherited sentiment of the philosopher, see Sjoerd van Tuinen "Populism and Grandeur: From Marx to Arafat," in *This Deleuzian Century: Art, Activism, Life,* eds. Rick Dolphijn and Rosi Braidotti, 87–114 (Amsterdam: Brill | Rodopi, 2014).

46 Deleuze and Guattari, *What Is Philosophy?*, 64–65.

thought), this plane must include not only repulsive concepts such as *ressentiment* and bad conscience, but also the pretensions of those who understand the will to power only from the point of view of nihilism. As a persona in the Nietzschean dramaturgy of *ressentiment*, the priest is the negative mirror image of the philosopher, a minimal power of imagination that immediately turns against its "author" by fixating the thought-movement in an empirical judgment.[47] But precisely by being affirmed as immanent, he is nonetheless integrated in a transcendental field of thought which, distributed over a proliferating plurality of irreducible and sometimes apparently mutually exclusive points of view, has a compelling and all the more powerful objective structure — a polemical and dramatic consistency — all of its own: "another always thinks in me, another who must also be thought."[48]

What orients us in this spastic schizophrenia of thought and distinguishes the philosopher from the priest cannot be the subjectivity or mentality of the thinker. Rather, what distinguishes them is their respective "pathos" and their mutual sympathies and antipathies. Whereas knowledge and ethics are already subjective manners of inhabiting and imagining the world, pathos precedes all subjectivity and constitutes the place in the world

47  Ibid., 65, 83.

48  Deleuze, *Difference and Repetition,* 199–200. Philosophy, Deleuze and
Guattari write, proceeds "blow by blow" (Deleuze and Guattari, *What Is
Philosophy?,* 76), in a constant combat with all the other personae that are
enfolded within its own plane of consistency. Hence philosophy's affinity
with schizophrenia, or the stammering of the Idiot as yet another persona
that forms an internal condition for the reality of a thought movement.
If the coherence of the drama is a witch's ride, the personae are the mari-
onettes of the philosopher's delirium. "I am no longer myself but thought's
aptitude for finding itself and spreading across a plane that passes through
me at several places. The philosopher is the idiosyncracy of his conceptual
personae. The destiny of the philosopher is to become his conceptual
persona or personae, at the same time that these personae themselves
become something other than what they are historically, mythologically or
commonly (the Socrates of Plato, the Dionysus of Nietzsche, the Idiot of
Nicholas of Cusa)" (ibid., 64, 70).

that the subject comes to occupy.[49] It is the singularly embodied experience that defines a perspective, the implicit condition for there to be any empirical fact at all; it is the "being-potential of the concept,"[50] an "instinctive, almost animal sapere — a *Fiat* or a *Fatum* that gives each philosopher the right of access to certain problems, like an imprint on his name or an affinity from which his works flow."[51] Whereas the priest, like a scientist, registers and knows *ressentiment* on the basis of its general recognizability or form and therefore lacks the taste for its relevance for the becoming of (a) life, the wisdom (*sapientia,* which Nietzsche equals to its etymological root in *sapio,* taste) of the philosopher consists of a taste for what is worthy of knowing (*wissenswürdig*).[52] "Philosophy does not consist in knowing and is not inspired by truth," as Deleuze and Guattari repeat in the manner of the pragmatists, "Rather, it is categories like Interesting, Remarkable, or Important that determine success or failure."[53] The criterion of thought is not adequacy to the given, but the efficacy of an act of thought that hierarchizes the given. The only criterion for its failure or success is the movement it

---

49  Friedrich Nietzsche, *The Gay Science: With a Prelude in Rhymes and an Appendix of Songs,* trans. Walter Kaufmann (New York: Vintage Books, 1974), 252.

50  Deleuze and Guattari, *What Is Philosophy?,* 69, 77–79.

51  Ibid., 79. Or as Deleuze wrote more than twenty years earlier: "There is something irreducible in the depths of the spirit: a monolithic bloc of Fatum, of decision already taken on all problems in their measure and their relation to us; and also a right that we have to accede to certain problems, like a hot-iron brand imprinted on our names" (Deleuze, *Difference and Repetition,* 200).

52  Friedrich Nietzsche, *Philosophy in the Tragic Age of the Greeks,* trans. Marianne Cowan (Chicago: Henry Regnery, 1962), 43.

53  Deleuze and Guattari, *What Is Philosophy?,* 82. Dramatization is therefore the method of philosophical pragmatism: "A true idea, in the pragmatic sense, is an idea that changes something in a satisfactory way in the mind of the person thinking it. The true idea is not only what one believes, does, or thinks; it is what makes us believe, makes us act or makes us think. Pragmatism is thus at the same time a method of evaluation of truth. [...] In effect, truth is now evaluated in function of a value that exceeds it: the Interesting" (David Lapoujade, *William James: Empirisme et pragmatisme* [Paris: Seuil, 2007], 74).

implies. Hence whereas the priest always speaks with calm reason, the philosopher's taste for exceptions finds its element in something that is all but reasonable.[54] If both the philosopher and the priest refer to the empirical fact of *ressentiment*, and yet only the former can lay claim to the full complexity of its problem, this is because he is inspired by a pathos of distance. Not only is there no *logos* without *pathos*; the philosophical *pathos* situates us within a *polemos,* that is, a rivalry of taste. Variety and conflict are not shortcomings of thought, but the original, primitive form of dramaturgy that belongs to philosophy and distinguishes it from its rivals. To formulate general rules and categories of thought, by contrast, already comes down to the end of taste. For this reason, dialectics, from Socrates to Hegel, is bad taste in philosophy.[55] Inspired precisely by the *pathos* of the priest, it is a taste for judgment, not for the problematization of becomings. Dialectics is never a real mediation as it reduces conflict to the general criteria of true knowledge, conflating the plane of immanence and the personae that occupy it within a propositional form without a real thought-movement. The taste of the philosopher, by contrast, acquires its validity and apodicticity only through its medial position, through enveloping into but also away from the competing becomings against which it has to be measured itself. Always beginning "from the middle," taking effect through shocks and proceeding in bursts, only the philosopher has the "power of decision"[56] to give *ressentiment* its proper name, even if the word has been abused by so many coming before or after him.[57]

---

54  Nietzsche, *Gay Science,* 77.

55  Deleuze and Guattari, *What Is Philosophy?,* 80.

56  Deleuze, *Difference and Repetition,* 199.

57  If the body is the domain of becomings before they are fixed by discourse and words, the task of the philosopher is to reach for the body and determine the consistency of its becomings, and thus give the body its first name. Cf. Gilles Deleuze, *Cinema 2: The Time-Image,* trans. Hugh Tomlinson and Robert Galeta (Minneapolis: University of Minnesota Press, 1989), 172–73.

In this sense of "[t]he lordly right of giving names,"[58] we may conclude that while the priest is the heteronym of Nietzsche, a character who thinks in Nietzsche, Nietzsche is only the pseudonym of the priest. The priest is a necessary co-pilot or wingman[59] in the flight of the concept surveying the plane of immanence, but he does not explain the becoming of Nietzschean philosophy. Whereas the priest consumes the concept of *ressentiment* as a psychological readymade (recognizing *ressentiment* everywhere) and reverses its critical sense (passing a moral judgment by identifying it with envy), he lacks the *pathos* that was necessary to invent the concept in the first place. While the philosopher offers the belief, orientation, or sense for combatting *ressentiment*, the priest merely possesses its truth and in this way continues morality, even in the criticism of morality itself.[60] Just as philosophy is folded over a sensual analogy, that *je ne sais quoi* that is the drama of the body in its silent and obscure becomings, the priest is its clear but confused abjection, the betrayal of the body's potential of becoming-other, or indeed, of the very justice and consistency of its passions. The priest, in other words, is the very embodiment of the risk of philosophy's moralization.

58 Nietzsche, *Genealogy of Morals,* 26.
59 Deleuze and Guattari, *What Is Philosophy?,* 78.
60 Nietzsche, *Genealogy of Morals,* 151–52.

# 5

# The Affective Economy: Producing and Consuming Affects in Deleuze and Guattari

*Jason Read*

The thought of Gilles Deleuze (and Félix Guattari) bears an ambiguous relation with respect to the "affective turn" in social and political thought that it supposedly helped initiate. This ambiguity touches on the very role and meaning of affects. From Deleuze's writings on Friedrich Nietzsche and Baruch Spinoza through the collaborations of *Capitalism and Schizophrenia,* Deleuze and Guattari insist on the central role of the affects, joy, sadness, fear, and hope, as structuring individual and collective life. In that sense, Deleuze and Guattari are rightfully hailed as central figures in a turn toward affect. However, if, as some argue, the "affective turn" is a turn toward the lived over the structural and the intimate over the public, then Deleuze and Guattari's thought has a much more complex relation to affects. The broader polemical target of Deleuze and Guattari's *Anti-Oedipus,* beyond the specific polemics with psychoanalysis, is any explanatory theory that would reduce social relations to expressions of individual passions and desires. Deleuze and Guattari's claim that there is only "desire and the social, and nothing else" is oriented against such individualistic accounts of not only social relations but subjectivity as well.[1] Moreover, Deleuze and Guattari's theory of capitalism argues that it reproduces itself in and through the encounter of abstract quantities of money and labor power, and as such is a social relation that is indifferent to the beliefs and meaning that we attach to it. Thus, if affect is central to Deleuze and Guattari's thought, it is necessary to add the caveats that affect must be thought of as anti-individualistic rather than individualistic, as social rather than intimate, and as impersonal, reflecting the abstractions that dominate life.

The caveats with respect to affect are as much strengths as they are limitations. Which is to say that it is not a matter of simply reconciling the concept of affect with Deleuze and Guattari's critiques of Oedipal explanations and theory of capital, but of producing a concept of affect which is both anti-individualistic and adequate to the real abstractions and structural complexities of contemporary capitalism. If affect is to be the basis of a critical theory of contemporary society it must be radically separated from individualist accounts of social relations, accounts that have become increasingly pervasive in a neoliberal self-help culture, on the one hand, and attuned to the "real abstractions" of contemporary capitalism, on the other. Affect must be a way of grasping the abstractions that determine individual and collective life, rather than a retreat into an interior free of them.

## Intensive affects and extensive emotions

Deleuze's engagement with affects is framed by two different philosophers: Spinoza and Gilbert Simondon. It was Spinoza who recognized both the ontological dimensions of affects, defining everything by its capacity to affect and be affected, and the political and social dimension of affects; they do not orient mere individual striving but do so only in and through the encounters and relations with others. Political collectives are

---

1    Gilles Deleuze and Félix Guattari, *Anti-Oedipus: Capitalism and Schizophrenia*, trans. Robert Hurley, Mark Seem, and Helen R. Lane (Minneapolis: University of Minnesota Press, 1983), 29.

defined more by common structures of feeling than common notions and ideas. The central task of politics, any politics, is then of organizing and defining the affects. Affects are thus necessarily both anti-humanist, defining all of existence in various ways, and transindividual, passing in and through relations with others. Deleuze's definition, or use of affects, exceeds Spinoza in that he adds another distinction: between the intensive order of affects and the extensive order of emotions. This definition is close to Simondon, as we will see below, for whom affects correspond to the intense and metastable dimension of existence, defined by tensions and transformations, while emotions are more defined and individuated. It is thus no surprise that this distinction has been read by affect theorists, such as Brian Massumi, to correspond to a distinction between affect, understood as an impersonal intensity, and emotion, understood as a subjectivized and individuated feeling. As Massumi writes:

> An emotion is a subjective content, the sociolinguistic fixing of the quality of an experience which is from that point onward defined as personal. Emotion is qualified intensity, the conventional, consensual point of insertion of intensity into semantically and semiotically formed progressions, into narrativizable action-reaction circuits, into function and meaning. It is intensity owned and recognized. It is crucial to theorize the difference between affect and emotion.[2]

While such a distinction may help orient Deleuze's thought of affect, it is completely absent from Spinoza's work. Spinoza's use of the term affect (*affectus* in Latin) is absolutely and rigorously consistent; affects define not only the different states of human subjective life, from the basic joy and sadness to the complex and ambivalent affects of jealousy and ambition, but define everything, every finite thing has a capacity to affect or be affected. Affects are less some uniquely human attribute, making us a

2   Brian Massumi, *Parables for the Virtual: Movement, Affect, Sensation* (Durham: Duke University Press, 2002), 28.

kingdom within a kingdom, but the general rule of existence; that of being modified or affected by encounters and relations, of which human life is only a particularly complex instance. For Spinoza we are constituted and individuated through our affects; the affective composition differs from individual to individual, but this individuation does not take the form of a distinction between affects and emotions.

Despite these terminological differences it is thus possible to understand affect in Deleuze as reconciling two different problems: Spinoza's emphasis on the political organization of affect, and Simondon's emphasis on affects as individuation. Simondon's thought is oriented around a central problematization of the individual. Individuation has to be considered as a process and not the default state of being. This process moves from a milieu that is considered pre-individual, made up of tensions and relations, to a process of individuation that increasingly encompasses different levels and aspects, biological, psychic, and social. The social is then not a negation of individuation, but its condition. Transindividuality lies in the fact that the social is not so much a suppression of individuality, a loss of the individual in the collective, but its transformation and condition. Within this relation the distinction between affect and emotion figures twice. First in that affects are less individuated than emotions; while emotions are the emotions of specific subjects relating to specific objects, affects constitute more of an inchoate sense or sensibility. Second in that affects are intensive while emotions are extensive. The passage from affects to emotions is part of general individuation, and as such it necessarily passes through the constitution of collectivity. As Simondon writes:

If one is able to speak in a certain sense of the individuality of a group or such and such a people, it is not by virtue of a community of action, too discontinuous to be a solid base, nor of the identity of conscious representations, too large and too continuous to permit the segregation of groups; it is at the level of affective-emotional themes, mixtures of representation and action, that constitute collective groups.[3]

The individuality of the collective, if it is to have any individuality at all, must be sought at the level of particular affects and emotions, particular ways of feeling and perceiving the world, which is often tied to particular objects. In place of the rigid distinction between affect and emotion, in which one is social, the other individual, Simondon argues that both individuals and collectives are constituted by affects and emotions. Individuals individuated as subjects and the individuation of collectivity, the constitution of definite collectives, are both constituted through the pre-individual dimension of affects, and their increasing individuation into emotional evaluations. Collectives are defined by their "structures of feeling."

Despite the terminological difference of affect and emotion, both Spinoza and Simondon see affect as something that passes between the pre-individual and the transindividual (even if these specific terms are missing from the former). For Simondon affects are part of the metastable milieu that remains, even as individual emotions and perceptions are constituted. The affective dimension carries over from the pre-individual constituting a kind of indetermination at the heart of individuation, an indetermination that demands a social dimension in order to be at least partially resolved. In a similar fashion, Spinoza's affects are pre-individual, they are less determinate states of individuals and properties of objects than passages and transformations, increases and decreases of power. Joy is nothing other than a passage from a lesser to a greater perfection and sadness is only the opposite. Affects are intensities, transformations of states, rather than determinate conditions. These states cannot be separated from their supposed opposites, from the ambivalence of the affects; sadness cannot be rigorously separated from joy, hate from love. As much as the affects are less determined

3   Gilbert Simondon, *L'individuation à la lumière des notions de forme et d'information* (Grenoble: Jérôme Million, 2005), 248.

states than an index of their transformation, initiating a process of the constitution and destruction of individuation, they are necessarily transindividual. Or, more to the point, it is because the affects are always situated in the increases and decreases of power that they are necessarily transindividual. For Simondon the progression of individuation that takes place between affects and emotions necessarily passes through the transindividual as affects coalesce around perceptual points of view and relations.[4] While in Spinoza it is not that one passes from the pre-individual affects to individuated emotions, but the basic affects of love and hate enter into increasingly individuated combinations as they shape the affective composition of an individual. As Spinoza writes, "each affect of each individual differs from the affect of another as much as the essence of one from the essence of the other."[5] The different essences are nothing other than the different compositions and combinations of affects. Affects and emotions are the transindividual intersection between individual and collective individuation.

The difference of terminology between affect and emotion risks obscuring other, more salient, differences between Simondon and Spinoza. Spinoza's relational account of the various affects is oriented around a fundamental distinction, the fundamental axiological distinction of an increase or decrease in power.[6] It is this distinction that initially distinguishes joy and sadness, and is carried over into the various permutations of love and hate. This is not to suggest that this duality constitutes some kind of core that all of the affects could be reduced to, so all that matters is joy or sadness, increase or decrease in power. There is a constitutive tension between the basic orientation of joy and sadness and the constitutive complexity of the myriad ways sadness and joy are combined and articulated. Second, this duality of joy and sadness is divided again in the split between

4   Simondon, *L'individuation,* 261.
5   Baruch Spinoza, *Ethics,* trans. Edwin Curley (London: Penguin Classics, 1996), III.P57.
6   Hasana Sharp, *Spinoza and the Politics of Renaturalization* (Chicago: University of Chicago Press, 2011), 40.

the joyful passive affects and the sad passive affects, between those affects which are joyful, reflecting an increase of power, but have an external cause, and those that have their own internal determination.[7] At the level of affects one divides into two. This complicates the initial axiology of joy and sadness, introducing the idea that there is a negative dimension to passive joys, a possibility that they can be excessive, and a positive dimension, or at the very least a utility, to such passive sad affects as fear and humility. Spinoza's definition of the affects is situated within the ethical horizon of becoming active.

Between Simondon and Spinoza we have the basic coordinates that orient Deleuze's thoughts on affect. Affects are situated within the process of collective and individual individuation, constituting the basis of both collective relations and individual subjectivity. The axis of the individual and collective is in turn bifurcated by the axis dividing the becoming active from becoming passive. Which is to argue that affects are the conditions of both subjection and transformation, situated between power and individuation.

## Consuming affects

*Anti-Oedipus,* the first of the two volumes of *Capitalism and Schizophrenia,* opens with a citation of the fundamental political question of Spinoza's work, "Why do men fight for their servitude as if it was salvation?"[8] Spinoza's answer to this question necessarily involves the affects of fear, ambition, and hope as they structure both political life and individual desires. Thus, it is somewhat odd to note that affect does not appear in *Anti-Oedipus,* at least by name. Affect appears between the lines in terms of both the general problems outlined above, and, more importantly, *Anti-Oedipus* shifts the basic problem of servitude

7   Laurent Bove, *La stratégie du conatus: affirmation et résistance chez Spinoza* (Paris: Vrin, 1996), 130.
8   Deleuze and Guattari, *Anti-Oedipus,* 29.

and salvation in Spinoza's thought from politics understood as the rule of tyranny to political economy.

In Anti-Oedipus, affect is introduced first under the name of *Stimmung,* or mood. While the term *Stimmung* suggests a reference to Martin Heidegger, who philosophers such as Étienne Balibar and Antonio Negri have recognized as the other, often opposed, philosopher of affect, the reference is to Nietzsche by way of Pierre Klossowski. Either way, the fundamental effect suggests a broader basis for a philosophy of affect. What ties these different and disparate philosophies together, is the assertion of the unavoidable affective or emotional dimension of all thought and practice, as a fundamentally orienting dimension of thought. Deleuze and Guattari situate *Stimmung,* the intensities of affect, with the third synthesis; that of conjunctive synthesis of consumption. A few provisional conclusions can be drawn from this placement (without necessarily engaging Deleuze and Guattari's entire reading of syntheses). First and foremost: affects are consumed and this consumption comes after the synthesis of the production and the recording of desire. Deleuze and Guattari locate the subject on this synthesis. The subject comes after the production of desire and the recording of desire, caught in the tension between the forces that constitute the world and their inscription. As Deleuze and Guattari write,

> Thus this subject consumes and consummates each of the states through which it passes, and is born of each of them anew, continuously emerging from them as a part made up of parts, each one of which completely fills up the body without organs in the space of an instant.[9]

Deleuze and Guattari's conception of subject can be compared to Spinoza's assertion that we do not want something because it is good, but we call it good because we want it, desire it, and strive for it. Our affects come after history, a history of produc-

9    Ibid., 41.

tion and recording, that determines them, and our awareness of affects comes even after that. Subjectivity is secondary to, and unaware of, the process that produces it. It is situated between desiring production and the body without organs, between the process of production and its product; a product that in turn appropriates the various processes of production. Phrased differently, we could say that affects, intensities are always situated between the process of individuation, the production and practices that produce and exceed individuation, and its product, the individual, between the conditions of individuation and individuation itself. Affect is the instability and tension of the relation of individuation and production, and as such it can always misrecognize its conditions. As Deleuze and Guattari cite one of Karl Marx's more prosaic statements, "we cannot tell from the mere taste of wheat who grew it; the product gives us no hint as to the system and the relations of production."[10] Deleuze and Guattari draw profound insights from this statement, connecting it to the idea of commodity fetishism, a process of production. This is the condition for Oedipal subjectivity; a subject that continually misrecognizes the condition of its production, seeing itself as the product of the family rather than the historical process which has produced it.

What does it mean to consume affect, or think of affect as consumption, and how does it relate to both the theory of capital and the critique of Oedipus? Deleuze and Guattari's particular rewriting of the distinction between pre-capitalist and capitalist economic formations focuses on the role of the family in social production and reproduction. As Deleuze and Guattari argue, the various social formations that precede capitalism all have as their defining characteristic the fact that the very relations that produce and reproduce individuals are directly intertwined with the praxis and politics of social reproduction. Familial relations are directly both political and economic. It is only in capitalism, in the massive privatization of desire, that there is a separation of reproduction from social production.

10  Ibid., 24.

Capital puts to work deterritorialized flows of labor; it is thus indifferent to the specific marking or memories of individuals. As Deleuze and Guattari write:

> The alliances and filiations no longer pass through people but through money; so the family becomes a microcosm, suited to expressing what it no longer dominates. In a certain sense the situation has not changed; for what is invested through the family is still the economic, political, and cultural social field, its breaks and flows. Private persons are an illusion, images of images or derivatives of derivatives.[11]

Of course the family still continues to reproduce social relations, but it does so, paradoxically, through its separation and privatization. The family becomes an intimate space that represents social relations rather than reproducing them, all of society is seen through the idea of the father and the mother. Presidents and dictators become father figures and nations become motherlands: all of history and society is folded back into the family. This representation is itself a kind of reproduction, but one that has been privatized and depoliticized because it is outside of the conditions of social production.

Capitalism is defined by social production that passes through axioms of abstract quantities, flows of money and labor that are the real relations of alliance and filiation, rather than codes. Codes have become private matters, searches for meaning. This split between production and reproduction constitutes a very particular affective relation as well, which Deleuze and Guattari summarize as, "the age of cynicism, accompanied by a strange piety. (The two taken together constitute humanism; cynicism is the physical immanence of the social field, and piety is the maintenance of a spiritualized Urstaat [...])."[12] These two affects, cynicism and piety, correspond to the division of social production and reproduction. In the first, in the axioms of capi-

11  Ibid., 264.
12  Ibid., 225.

tal, we have a social order that reproduces itself without meaning or code. Axioms merely set up a relation between two quantities, a flow of labor and a flow of money. One does not believe in, or justify, the rate at which labor is exchanged for money — it simply is. Cynicism is an affect attuned to the indifference of the axioms that produce and reproduce social life, the recognition that the flows of the market mean nothing, have no justification, than their brute effectivity. Piety is reserved for the home, for the intimate sphere of reproduction that becomes the source of all the pleasure and pain. Capitalism's affective economy of cynicism and piety is thus distinguished from the savage economy of cruelty and the barbarian economy of fear, both of which were public despite all of their cruelties. Deleuze and Guattari's division of affective life between cynicism and piety is given a contemporary update by Paolo Virno, who writes:

> It is no accident, therefore, that the most brazen cynicism is accompanied by unrestrained sentimentalism. The vital contents of emotion — excluded from the inventories of an experience that is above all else an experience of formalisms and abstractions — secretly returns simplified and unelaborated, as arrogant as they are puerile. Nothing is more common than the mass media technician who after a hard day at work, goes off to the movies and cries.[13]

What connects these two theories of affect in contemporary society is that what is depleted from any affective investment in public life, in the activities of work and politics, returns in private life.

What ties together cynicism and piety, indifference and sentimentality, is that each affect is passive. These affects are passive in two senses. First, the conditions of their production are elsewhere, outside of the familial space in which they are produced.

---

13  Paolo Virno, "The Ambivalence of Disenchantment," trans. Michael Turits, in *Radical Thought in Italy: A Potential Politics,* eds. Michael Hardt and Paolo Virno, 13–34 (Minneapolis: University of Minnesota, 2006), 18.

Secondly, the conditions of the production of affects cannot be acted on. The axioms remain outside the sphere of politics, of individual and collective action. They are each passive, but in different senses. Cynicism, the affect attached to the working of the economy, confronts an economy that is perceived as being indifferent to human actions, while piety attaches itself to the family, which is perceived as being absolutely ahistorical. Far from seeing the privatization of desire and affects as liberation, as setting it free from the collective structures and relations, Deleuze and Guattari see the privatization as their subjection. To be passive is to be acted on, without acting in turn. The Spinozist critique of passivity is coupled with Marx's critique of fetishism: it is not just that we are passive in the face of the structures and relations that determine us, but unable to comprehend them, relating them back to ideal representations, the family, the father's love, rather than material conditions. Representation, especially the representation that passes through the interiorized conflicts and codes of the family, making the entire outside world an allegory for it, is the ultimate repression of production, of the productive powers of desire.

The genealogy of Oedipus is one in which intensity, what Deleuze and Guattari refer to as the "immense germinal flow," desiring production in all of its multiple connections and multivalent associations, is eventually interiorized, extended into representations. The process begins in the first coding of desire, the mnemotechnics that breed and constitute a "man that can keep promises," and culminates in the private home. Affects have lost their intensity, their productivity and multiplicity, to become grounded in the family, to become representations of the world rather than its production. There is nonetheless a tension in *Anti-Oedipus* between a genealogy of the specific affects of cynicism and piety, affects that reflect the split between production and reproduction in capitalism, and a general critique of the reduction of the entire level of affect to consumption and representation, the reduction of intensity to extension, and production to representation. In the former the rise of Oedipus and capital is associated with particular "sad affects"; those of cynicism and piety, while in the latter it is a matter of not so much the particular constitution of affects, than a general reduction of affects to consumption, to representation, and privatization.

## Capturing affects

Of the many conceptual and rhetorical changes that underlie the shift from *Anti-Oedipus* to *A Thousand Plateaus,* perhaps one of the most striking is the loss of Oedipus as a target of critique. The elimination of the entire polemic against Sigmund Freud and psychoanalysis shifts fundamentally the status of affect. Affect is no longer associated with consumption, and thus with the privatization of desire, but part of a general dimension of the micropolitics of society. The ninth plateau on "Micro-Politics of Segmentary" resumes some of the central themes of *Anti-Oedipus*'s social theory, only now they are presented less as a genealogy of Oedipal subjectivity and more as a general theory of the micro-politics of all of society.

The first task of any such theory is to differentiate between the molecular and the molar. These terms do not address scale, with the molecular constituting the private spaces of home or family, and the molar addressing the state and its institutions. The molecular is not more individual than the molar, and the molar is not more collective than the molecular. Rather, the molecular and the molar constantly intersect at all levels of society and subjectivity, framing two different ways of perceiving, two different politics. As Deleuze and Guattari write:

In short, everything is political, but every politics is simultaneously a *macropolitics* and a *micropolitics.* Take aggregates of the perception or feeling type: their molar organization, their rigid segmentarity, does not preclude the existence of an entire world of unconscious micropercepts, unconscious affects, fine segmentations that grasp or experience different things, are distributed and operate differently. There is a micropolitics of perception, affection, conversation, and so forth.[14]

The terminology of the molecular and the molar was already at work in *Anti-Oedipus,* specifically in the final, programmatic section dedicated to schizoanalysis, but it operated in tension with the genealogy of Oedipus, and an ironic conception of history in which savagery, barbarism, and capitalism culminate in Oedipus, a kind of motley painting of everything ever believed.

*A Thousand Plateaus* could be understood as a culmination of the positive project of schizonanalysis over the polemical one, as the critique of Oedipus, of psychoanalysis, which gives way to the construction of an ontology and politics of assemblages, a nomadic politics. It is in many ways an an-Oedipal book rather than an anti-Oedipal book, which not only does not need to kill any fathers — Oedipus, Freud, Jacques Lacan — but also no longer pays tribute to any lineage, any filiation. In place of the multiple debts to Marx, Nietzsche, and even Antonin Artaud and Franz Kafka, we get a series of nomadic borrowings and deterritorializations from various fields and disciplines from ancient history to ethology and the study of birdsongs. While such a distinction captures much of the shift of tone and style between the books, it does not fully capture what is at stake. Eduardo Viveiros de Castro has offered two points of reorientation that shed light on the shift between the two volumes. The first is the shift from production to becoming. As Viveiros de Castro argues: "The concept of becoming effectively plays the same axial cosmological role in *A Thousand Plateaus* that the concept of production plays in *Anti-Oedipus*."[15] Desiring production is replaced by the various becomings, woman, animal, etc. This shift from production to becoming marks another shift, one in which filiation is no longer the privileged term of an ontology of social

14  Gilles Deleuze and Félix Guattari, *A Thousand Plateaus: Capitalism and Schizophrenia,* trans. Brian Massumi (Minneapolis: University of Minnesota Press, 1987), 213.

15  Eduardo Viveiros de Castro, *Métaphysiques Cannibales* (Paris: Presses Universitaire de France, 2009), 133.

relations, but alliance takes its place. In the first volume, filiation, the intense germinal influx of desire and production, was what every society must repress, and emerges in the productive capacity of capital. Alliance is always the inscription, the coding of this intensity into determinant subjects goals and desires. It is only once filiation is coupled with alliance that we get social reproduction, the rule of the relations of production over the forces of production. While in the second volume it is alliance, the alliances between humans and animals, the nomads and the outside, that constitutes the basis for becoming and transformation. Filiation, the lines of descent, are always those of the state, of memory and authority. This shift could be understood as a shift of critical targets, even politics, from the critique of capital, which appropriates the power of filiation, appearing as the quasi-cause of capitalist production, to the critique of the state, which subordinates alliance to the state as a condition of belonging. The task of *Anti-Oedipus* was to think a production irreducible to teleological and instrumental logics of production, breaking production from the "mirror of production," while the task of *A Thousand Plateaus* (at least some of the latter plateaus) is to think exchange irreducible to possessive individualistic foundations of the social order. Thus, the first volume endeavored to break the production, an intensive filiation, free from its subordination to the inscription of dominant orders and relations, the domination of dead labor over the living, while the second endeavors to break alliance, an alliance of becoming, free from the filiation of the state. There is a general shift of valorized terms from production and filiation to becoming and alliance, a shift which has ontological and political effects.

Returning to the question of affect, it is now possible to ask what do these shifts of focus, alliance and filiation, production and becoming, relate to, and resituate the idea of affect. We have already seen how *Anti-Oedipus* juxtaposes the productive nature of desire, of affect, from its consumption in the family, effectively drawing a line of demarcation between two filiations, one intensive and productive, the other extensive and consumptive. What line of demarcation separates becoming from alliance organized under the categories of the state? For Deleuze and Guattari this distinction has to do with an apparatus of capture. An apparatus of capture functions through two terms, through direct comparison and monopolistic appropriation.[16] Direct comparison reduces the various activities to one homogenous activity in the case of labor, or the various objects to instances of one homogenous object in the case of the commodity. Monopolistic appropriation, on the other hand, is not a secondary accumulation imposed upon this comparison but its necessary precondition. As Deleuze and Guattari write:

> Surplus labor is not that which exceeds labor; on the contrary, labor is that which is subtracted from surplus labor and presupposes it. It is only in this context that one may speak of labor value, and of an evaluation bearing on the quantity of social labor, whereas primitive groups were under a regime of free action or activity in continuous variation.[17]

It is the monopoly, the appropriation by force, which constitutes the very ground for the comparison of different activities, different objects, making them interchangeable.

The point of contrast to this apparatus of capture is becoming. Becoming establishes a relation, between man and woman, humanity and animals, but it is never a relation predicated on a shared identity, is never an exchange. "A becoming is not a correspondence between relations. But neither is it a resemblance, an imitation, or, at the limit, an identification."[18] A becoming is a transformation, but not one that passes in and through discernible identities, not a matter of some thing becoming some thing else, but is a transformation at the level of the pre-individual, a reorganization at the level of the very conditions of individuation. If capture passes through hierarchy and identity, revealing the secret unity that connects identity to hierarchy,

16  Deleuze and Guattari, *A Thousand Plateaus,* 444.
17  Ibid., 442.
18  Ibid., 237.

then becoming passes through immanence and transformation, undoing both identity and hierarchy. This is why becomings pass through the very hierarchies that place men above women, humans above animals, undoing them by challenging the very identity of man and woman, human and animal. The examples of becoming are drawn from the history and mythology of transformations, where humans take on the qualities of animals and vice versa, transformations that exceed imitation or resemblance. Becomings are alliances, but strange alliances that constitute neither resemblance nor identity. The apparatus of capture makes the disparate similar by subjecting them to the same standard and the same rule; in contrast to this, becoming makes the similar different, even from itself, undoing all standards and all hierarchies of comparison.

It is in this context, in the distinction between capture/ exchange and becoming, that we get a definition of affect. As Deleuze and Guattari write, "For the affect is not a personal feeling, nor is it a characteristic; it is the effectuation of a power of the pack that throws the self into upheaval and makes it reel."[19] Affects are tied to becomings, to transformations. If we then wanted to think of affects in terms of an opposition to emotions, it is possible to argue that emotions are affects rendered comparable and exchangeable. Thus, we could place affects and emotions alongside the opposition between free action and work, in which the second term is the comparison and capture of the latter. Emotions, then, are not only more individuated, more discrete and determined, they are comparable and more exchangeable. From this perspective to have an emotion is to have a determinate feeling (sadness, joy, etc.), while affects are less discernible feelings than indices of transformation. These discernible emotions constitute a common point of comparison, a common ground of experience between interchangeable subjects. Despite the fact that Spinoza argued that there are as many loves and hates as there are objects to love and hate, and as many lovers and haters, revealing the nominalist multiplic-

19  Ibid., 240.

ity underlying the oppositions of love and hate, we continue to speak of love and hate, jealousy and envy, as if they were always the same thing, constituting a common ground of comparison and experience. It would also be possible to argue that these two different organizations of feeling refer to two fundamentally different planes: on the first, that of affects, there are only relations of movement, change and transformation, while on the second, that of emotions, there is always a reference to a hidden plane of transcendence. Emotions always seem to refer us back to some transcendent idea of human nature, an idea that is all the more pernicious in remaining entirely hidden.

The opposition between affect and emotion then would refer back to the underlying opposition of Deleuze and Guattari's work, the opposition between immanence and transcendence. Fredric Jameson has criticized Deleuze and Guattari, especially the later Deleuze and Guattari of *A Thousand Plateaus,* of departing the material analysis of the production of desire for an increasingly moral distinction between concepts such as virtual/actual, immanent/transcendent.[20] However, this opposition is less a stark binary between good and bad terms that one can select or choose, than it is a relation of production and representation, organization and its capture. It is necessary to see the hierarchy and transcendence that constitutes the apparatus of capture as nothing other than a product of the organization of immanent relations. Frédéric Lordon and André Orléan have coined the term "immanent transcendence" to characterize the production of the transcendent by the immanent.[21] Their primary point of reference is Spinoza, whose ethics and politics could be understood as an examination of how it is that the organization of striving produces multiple ideals of transcendence, from

20 Fredric Jameson, "Marxism and Dualism in Deleuze," *The South Atlantic Quarterly* 96, no. 3, special edition *A Deleuzian Century?,* ed. Ian Buchanan (1997): 393–416, at 411.

21 Frédéric Lordon and André Orléan, "Genèse de l'État et Genèse de la monnaie: le modele de la potential multitudios," in *Spinoza et les sciences sociales,* eds. Yves Citton and Frédéric Lordon, 203–305 (Paris: Éditions Amsterdam, 2008), 246.

the state to God. These are not empty illusions, but actually reorganizations of desire functioning like feedback loops — the points of resonance that Deleuze and Guattari discuss. We organize our lives around these concepts, making them effectively true. The same point could be raised with respect to emotions; once an affect is labeled, recognized, and made a common point of comparison, it functions as an ordering principle for future affects. Affects become the raw material for a socially recognized system of emotions. From this perspective it then becomes even easier to relate these affects to "ideal" and transcendent modes of causation — the taste of wheat tells us nothing of the conditions that have produced it.

Such a reading of the distinction between emotion and affect corresponds to the shift in the definition and deployment of axioms in the second volume of *Capitalism and Schizophrenia*. In the first volume axioms were stressed in terms of their indifference to meaning and belief as social reproduction was in some sense divorced from the reproduction of the family. Axioms were juxtaposed to both the collective meaning of codes and the private meaning of recoding. The affective tenor of axioms was that of cynicism, of an indifference to meaning and belief. This affective evacuation was coupled with the recoding of various forms of piety and nostalgia. In the second volume, however, the emphasis shifts from an opposition between axioms and codes to one internal to axioms; it is an opposition between the denumerable sets that axioms act on and manipulate, and the nondenumerable sets that exceed them. As Deleuze and Guattari write:

> What characterizes the nondenumerable is neither the set nor its elements; rather, it is the connection, the "and" produced between elements, between sets, and which belongs to neither, which eludes them and constitutes a line of flight. The axiomatic manipulates only denumerable sets, even infinite ones, whereas the minorities constitute "fuzzy," non-

denumerable, nonaxiomizable sets, in short, "masses," multiplicities of escape and flux.[22]

The nondenumerable relates to the becomings that exceed capture and subjectification. Axioms can be added or subtracted for every identity, but cannot contend with the passages and transformations which exceed identity. Affects are the moments of transformation, the increases and decreases of power that pass between the determinable and identifiable emotions; they are pre-individuated, to use Simondon's terminology, or ambivalent in Spinoza's sense. Affects exceed the defined and denumerable states. However, as such they risk being simply epiphenomenal, vanishing moments of transformation that pass between determinate states.

The opposition of affect and emotion then returns us to what could be considered the question of revolution as understood by Deleuze and Guattari. It is not a matter of consolidating all of these various affects and intensities of change and transformation into a new code or axiom, referring them back to some higher unity of organization, but of constituting a politics of becoming, a minor politics of transformative possibilities. In *Anti-Oedipus* there was a search for the figure of this transformation, the schizo, the revolutionary etc., while *A Thousand Plateaus* searches for the nomad, the minority, the becomings that pass beneath identities and relations. The overall project remains fundamentally the same. However, there is a difference in that the first book gives this rupture a subjective figure, even a persona, hence the "schizo," while in the second the schizo not only disappears almost entirely, but the emphasis is on the minority, the becoming, that which exceeds representation and axiomatization. This difference of focus could be seen as something an improvement, removing the awkwardness of arguing for something that could be considered pro-schizophrenia. The minor politics of the nondenumerable set avoid such awkward identifications. However, the difference of focus also raises the

22  Deleuze and Guattari, *A Thousand Plateaus,* 470.

question as to what extent a politics can bypass figures, codes, and emotions altogether? Is it possible to constitute a politics of affects that would not require reterritorialization in new emotions, a new structure of feeling.

## Affective consumptions and productions

The concept of affect and its attendant concepts and provocations shift in the two volumes of *Capitalism and Schizophrenia*. In the first, the genealogy of affect pivots around a central conceptual opposition, that between production and consumption, but this general distinction between production and consumption, also constitutes a specific genealogy of affects, of the cynicism and piety that constitute the affective composition of capital. In the latter volume, the conceptual distinction shifts from production and consumption to becoming and its capture, and the genealogy of affects, to an opposition between affects, understood as indices of transformation, and emotions, understood as determined and subject to capture. History gives way to categorical distinctions, even a morality of good and bad. This is Jameson's critique.

Rather than read the transitions and transpositions of affect from *Anti-Oedipus* to *A Thousand Plateaus* as either a linear trajectory of improvement, in which the concept is developed, or denigration, in which original insights are lost, I prefer to read the two different texts as each posing distinct and different problems. These different problems can be understood as a genealogy of affects in the first text, in which each particular epoch or era of social production can be considered to have a dominant affect, or affects. In this case cynicism and piety, rationalism and sentimentality, are the particular affective composition of capital, of a mode of production defined by the separation of production and reproduction. (To which I could add, but it really deserves more than a parenthesis, that these two different tasks constitute a gendered division of labor, with the gendering of cynicism as the masculine affect par excellence, while sentimentality is feminized. This division cuts through culture as well as economy, constituting various genres of entertainment, from cynical anti-heroes of action films to the sentimentality of lifetime movies.) There is much to be said for such an understanding of contemporary capital, making it possible to understand not only the current fatalism that defines economics but also the sentimentality that defines contemporary politics. From this perspective political candidates can be understood by precisely how they articulate and embody this combination of cynicism and sentimentality, deferring to the market while posing for the right photo ops, and shedding tears at the right moment. However, such a division also risks being too historicist, too oriented toward a hegemonic structure of feeling. Against this conception *A Thousand Plateaus* provides a necessary corrective. The later volume's emphasis on affect as the outside of emotion makes it possible to label the hegemonic structures of feelings as emotions, as recognized, comparable, and public structures of feeling, reserving the term "affect" for the transformations that pass between and under these states, never being named or conceptualized. It is through these affects that change happens, not just the change of passing from one emotion to another, but becoming, the transformations that disrupt and undo the existing emotional order.

The first offers us a history of affects, a history that situates affects within the divide between axiom and code, the abstractions that govern life and the codings that constitute its experience, while the second posits affects in terms of their untimely becomings that exceed historical determination. Both are required to not only make sense of the stabilizations and uncertainties of the present moment, but to ultimately transform it. In order to change the present it is necessary to identify the dominant structures of feeling, the cynicism and sentimentalisms, but also to trace the affects and becomings that pass between them, that constitute a new sensibility dwelling in the heart of the old.

6

# Deleuze's Transformation of the
# Ideology–Critique Project:
# Noology Critique

*Benoît Dillet*

> [*A concept*] *has nothing to do with ideology. A concept is full*
> *of critical and political force of liberty. It is precisely its power*
> *as a system that brings out what is good or bad, what is or*
> *is not new, what is or is not alive in a group of concepts.*
> — Gilles Deleuze[1]

*Introduction: Ideology... what ideology?*

Fifty years after the publication of *Reading Capital* by Louis Althusser and his students, the political landscape is unrecogniz-
able. We are immersed in economic parlance, from politicians,
experts, and intellectuals: everyone claims to know best how to
control the deficit, how to regulate the banking systems, how to
stop the flows of tax evasion, etc. Although the press has perhaps been too quick at pointing out the resurgence of Karl Marx
and Marxist thought in the wake of the economic crisis, we are
nonetheless witnessing a certain turn to political economy in
continental philosophy. It is as if critical theory had forgotten

1   Gilles Deleuze, *Negotiations: 1972–1990*, trans. Martin Joughin (New York:
    Columbia University Press, 195), 32.

about the economic order and on waking up to a totally dis-
organized and deeply unequal world, it suddenly found itself
being accused by some of being compromised by the capitalist
machinery, and by others as being speculative or naive. But this
situation is hardly new; the end of the 1970s — with the rise of
a discourse against the "totalitarian left" and preparations for
the neoliberal shock therapies — also saw a resurgence of the
problems of economic reason and ideology. When we charge
critical theory of being compromised by putting forward creativity or acceleration as the ideology of neoliberal capitalism, we
denounce (or regret) that ideology was not taken into account.
Pierre Macherey notes that Michel Foucault's conscious distancing from Marxist parlance meant that "the concept [of ideol-
ogy] did not have to be taken into account"[2] since it had lost
its substance, its facility to diagnose 1970s' political economy.
Instead, Foucault deliberately wanted to create new concepts to
overcome the Marxist regime of discourse. Not simply to reject
the predominance of capital over labor, but to supplement the
analysis with a more refined understanding of political reality (discipline, governmentality, and biopolitics). Furthermore,
Foucault aimed to move away from the ideology/science dialectic, dominant in the French left in the 1960s–1970s.[3] I argue that
the discussion of ideology is not only implicitly present in the
work of Foucault and that of Gilles Deleuze and Félix Guattari,

2   Pierre Macherey, *Le sujet des normes* (Paris: Éditions Amsterdam, 2014),
    216.
3   In the section entitled "Knowledge [*savoir*] and ideology" in *Archaeology
    of Knowledge,* Foucault attempted to overcome explicitly this opposition.
    "It can be said that political economy has a role in capitalist society, that
    it serves the interests of the bourgeois class, that it was made by and for
    that class" or "ideology is not exclusive of scientificity" (Michel Foucault,
    *Archaeology of Knowledge,* trans. Alan M. Sheridan Smith [London: Rout-
    ledge, 2002], 204, 205). Étienne Balibar comments on Marx's difficulty in
    seeing the "Bourgeois political economy" as ideology given its scientificity
    (and the absence of abstraction or inverted reality), but Marx overcame
    this difficulty by writing "a critique of political economy." See Étienne
    Balibar, *The Philosophy of Marx,* trans. Chris Turner (London/New York:
    Verso Books, 2007), 54–6.

but a central aspect of their work. In order to do so I reconstruct their position vis-à-vis ideology to understand more broadly their engagement with political economy and the critique of the images of capitalism.

By contrasting too starkly between the subjective (ideology) and the objective (science), the irrational and the rational, political economy fails to take into account the production of desire in capitalism. This is problematic, since the abstraction of desire — taking place alongside the abstraction of labor — should not be taken for granted but rather be put at the center of a renewed ideology critique. By integrating desire with the infrastructure, "[l]ibidinal economy is no less objective than political economy," write Deleuze and Guattari.[4] To establish a libidinal economy is another way of doing a critique of political economy and demonstrating the noological production of science, without falling into the extreme opposite position that places desire as the irrational force to be celebrated:

[t]here is an unconscious libidinal investment of desire that does not necessarily coincide with the preconscious investments of interest, and that explains how the latter can be perturbed and perverted in "the darkest organization," below all ideology.[5]

The darkest organization here is what I want to revisit as "noology," and I will define this project as the re-materialization of ideology critique.

My interpretation of Deleuze and Guattari's work here follows and complements Macherey's recent studies on ideology that attempt *to think ideology today* (by reading Foucault), that is, when after Daniel Bell and others, the end of ideology was

4   Gilles Deleuze and Félix Guattari, *Anti-Oedipus: Capitalism and Schizophrenia,* trans. Robert Hurley, Mark Seem, and Helen R. Lane (Minneapolis: University of Minnesota Press, 1983), 345.

5   Ibid., translation modified.

proclaimed.[6] Macherey's position is particularly interesting since he does not want to discard this disappearance of ideology and instead makes a parallel between the discourse on the end of ideology and Foucault's work on the society of norms. Ideology has become both ubiquitous and imperceptible, and critics have either given up in front of ideology since it is most adaptable, invisible, and indiscernible, or worse they have also believed that ideology had vanished, as if contemporary societies were post-capitalist and post-materialist. Macherey's rhetorical question is: "is only a society without ideology possible?"[7] In asking this question and arguing for the persistence of the theme of ideology, he does not claim that society should be or can be without ideology, but that the problem is not posed correctly. It should be posed in terms of normalization and discipline rather than ideology and repression.

As Alberto Toscano has recently argued (following Guillaume Sibertin-Blanc), the new concepts introduced by Foucault often supplement the Marxist critique of political economy: it is capital that conditions biopolitics, and therefore requires "a revision in the very notion of 'ideology.'"[8] Deleuze and Guattari understood this move very early on and integrated it into their work. They argue that alienation and subjection should not be understood in terms of ideology and ideological structures, but by drawing the diagrams of the technologies of power and the emergence of the normalizing power. For instance, in 1973, they explain:

> Ideology has no importance here: what matters is not ideology, and not even the "economic/ideological" distinction or

6   Pierre Macherey, *Études de philosophie "française": De Sieyes à Barni* (Paris: Publications de la Sorbonne, 2013), 63–110; Macherey, *Le sujet des normes,* 213–352.

7   Macherey, *Études,* 96.

8   Alberto Toscano, "What Is Capitalist Power? Reflections on 'Truth and Juridical Forms,'" in *Foucault and the History of Our Present,* eds. Sophie Fuggle, Yari Lanci, and Martina Tazzioli, 26–42 (Basingstoke: Palgrave Macmillan, 2015), 33.

opposition; what matters is the organization of power. Because the *organization of power,* i.e., the way in which desire is already in the economic, the way libido invests the economic, haunts the economic and fosters the political forms of repression.[9]

For them, ideology as understood and commonly used by Marxists in the 1960s and 1970s prevented an understanding of the organization of power, the becoming-state of all organizations, and particularly that of the French Communist Party (PCF) that aspired to duplicate and replicate the Soviet Communist Party apparatus by using its scientific propositions. For Deleuze and Guattari, the Marxist use of infrastructure (the material condition) and superstructure (culture, ideas, desire, and ideology) prevents the integration of desire and affects into a critique of political economy, when diagnosing the material constitution of humans, particularly in relation to employment and work. They briefly introduced the concept of "noology" at the end of *A Thousand Plateaus,* in the 12th and 14th plateaus, almost as an afterthought, to leave the book as an open book and an open system: "Noology, which is distinct from ideology, is precisely the study of images of thought, and their historicity."[10]

A noological model is concerned not with thought contents (ideology) but with the form, manner or mode, and function of thought, according to the mental space it draws and from the point of view of a general theory of thought, a thinking of thought.[11]

9   Gilles Deleuze and Félix Guattari, *Desert Islands and Other Texts: 1953–1974,* ed. David Lapoujade, trans. Michael Taormina (Los Angeles: Semiotext(e), 2004), 263, emphasis in the original.

10  Gilles Deleuze and Félix Guattari, *A Thousand Plateaus: Capitalism and Schizophrenia,* trans. Brian Massumi (Minneapolis: University of Minnesota Press, 1987), 376.

11  Ibid., 499–500.

It is not what one thinks or what a class thinks that matters, but how they think it, in what assemblages thought takes place, and for what purpose. For the moment, it is enough to remark that they intend to collapse the two-level analysis of ideology critique, and rather analyze the wiring of thought. I will unpack these two quotations along two lines: first by showing that Deleuze and Guattari did not radically discard ideology-critique but transformed it by adding new problems (particularly that of affects and desire), and second, by pointing to the potentials of a noology critique, when we understand noology as a re-materialized understanding of ideology.[12] Although I am taking these two quotations from *A Thousand Plateaus* as the starting point of my argument, I will mostly focus on *Anti-Oedipus* and the critique of familialism in this essay to show their engagement in ideology critique.

To introduce the context of noology critique as their transformation of ideology critique, we need to note that for Deleuze and Guattari, it is on the one hand a continuation of the project of the reversal of Platonism started by Deleuze in *Difference and Repetition,* but on the other hand to resist an anti-Platonism that is equally idealist — placing thought above everything else, before the body, a thought without the body but also a body without thoughts, or a body without organs. The increasing forms of mental alienation today, linked to a cognitive and affective capitalism, have only furthered the division of mental and physical labor rather than abolished it. Everyone is a proletarian, and by using the expression "proletarian ideology," Marx-

12 This is also what Fredric Jameson perceived in his chapter on Deleuze: the noology critique project is to expose the ideology of dualism (and Jameson finds the contemporary resurgence of ethics as a specialized discipline as paradigmatic). See Fredric Jameson, *Valences of the Dialectic* (London/New York: Verso Books, 2009), 181–200. Another contribution worth signaling is Jason Read's brilliant article on noology that focuses on commodity fetishism and abstract labor. Read is in dialogue with Marx's later work (when the thematic of commodity fetishism replaces that of ideology). See Jason Read, "The Fetish is Always Actual, Revolution is Always Virtual: From Noology to Noopolitics," *Deleuze Studies* 3, supplement (2009): 78–101.

ists have largely displaced the meaning and the role of ideology. Marx and Friedrich Engels never used this expression since the very concept of ideology always already refers to the dominant "worldview."[13] I simplify a much longer story here, but this "vacillation" of the concept of ideology led many Marxists to adopt largely idealist views.[14] To take one example out of many, we can refer to the Marxist cinema historian, Georges Sadoul, as commented on by André Bazin. Bazin notes that in writing about the origins of cinema, Sadoul had forgotten about the technical invention of cinema and argued for "a reversal of the historical order of causality, which goes from the economic infrastructure to the ideological superstructure,"[15] as if "cinema is an idealistic phenomenon. The concept men had of it existed so to speak fully armed in their minds, as if in some platonic heaven [...]."[16] The idealist use of ideology consists here in thinking that ideas invented cinema and that scientists and technicians had almost no role to play, that cinema was not born in the experiments with technical objects. The idealist conception of ideology reduced ideology-critique to a battle of ideas, forgetting the affective and the material formation of ideology itself.

13  Étienne Balibar makes this important point that historically the "proletarian worldview" is "inseparable from the goal of constructing a party," that is an institution with a formal structure, and not simply some vague ideas of class consciousness (that is also absent from Marx). Yet can any party exist without a general theory of thought? (Étienne Balibar, *Masses, Classes, Ideas: Studies on Politics and Philosophy Before and After Marx,* trans. James Swenson [London: Routledge, 1994], 153).

14  "The current uses of the term ideology, Marxist and non-Marxist [...] tend to fall back to one side or other of a classic demarcation line between the theoretical [...] and the practical" (Étienne Balibar, *The Philosophy of Marx,* trans. Chris Turner [London/New York: Verso Books, 2007], 45).

15  André Bazin, *What is Cinema?,* vol. 1, trans. Hugh Gray (Berkeley: University of California Press, 2005), 17.

16  Ibid.

## Ideology is dead, long live noology!

I want to propose the hypothesis that the notion of noology is useful to understand the transformation, rather than the denial, of ideology during the 1970s and 1980s in the work of Deleuze and Guattari. A crucial aspect of this transformation is their insistence that "*desire is part of the infrastructure.*"[17] The significance of this statement and what it implies can be summed up in two points. First, Deleuze and Guattari attempted in *Anti-Oedipus* to supplement the critique of political economy with a critique of libidinal economy, yet they are cautious to note that these should not be confounded and merged, but that their differentiating investments should be integrated into the analysis. I argue, largely following Macherey, that by integrating desire into the infrastructure, they intend to flatten or collapse the infrastructure/superstructure in order to re-materialize ideology critique (as noology critique). The second point is that Deleuze and Guattari want to save desire from ideology, and show that in fact there is an economy of desire, or that desire is part of the economy. They explicitly refer to Pierre Klossowski's *The Living Currency* (1970) on this point, to make evident the association of desire with ideology ("two kinds of fantasy"), for desire, drives and affects "creat[e] within the economic forms their own repression, as well as the means for breaking this repression."[18]

17  Deleuze and Guattari, *Anti-Oedipus,* 104. This is again emphasized in an interview, see Gilles Deleuze and Félix Guattari, "On Anti-Oedipus," in Deleuze, *Negotiations*, 19. Frédéric Lordon has recently developed this problem forcefully in *Willing Slaves of Capital: Spinoza and Marx of Desire,* trans. Gabriel Ash (London/New York: Verso Books, 2014). For Lordon, the desires of the workers are captured by the "master-desire" of the employers. Even though Lordon makes clear that the bosses (patrons) are not only employers, and so the worker-employer opposition found in this book for the most part differs from Deleuze and Guattari's understanding of the production of desire.

18  Deleuze and Guattari, *Anti-Oedipus,* 63. See also, Pierre Klossowski, *The Living Currency,* trans. Daniel W. Smith, Vernon W. Cisney, and Nicolae Morar (London: Bloomsbury, forthcoming 2016).

Readers of *A Thousand Plateaus* will certainly remember the bold and provocative statement "there is no ideology and never has been."[19] Yet, far from denying ideology itself this statement was intended to be performative and dramatic, much like a slogan, as Robert Porter has astutely described it.[20] As we will see further, for Deleuze and Guattari, once ideology is transformed into "noology," the power relations and the technical wiring of thought become evident and the evasive understanding of ideology as "ideology-cloud"[21] disappears. This transformation is made possible by integrating Foucault's work, as a point of no return, but also by continuing the critique of images of thought that occupied a central place in Deleuze's early work from *Nietzsche and Philosophy* to *Difference and Repetition*, and later in *Cinema 2: Time-Image* and *What Is Philosophy?*. In the English preface to *Difference and Repetition* written in 1986, Deleuze adds that the project of the image of thought (noology) remains for him "the most necessary and the most concrete."[22] In *What Is Philosophy?*, Deleuze and Guattari conclude that the image of thought is the plane of immanence, it is the image of "what it means to think" and the image of "the uses of thought" in a particular society at a given moment: "[t]he image of thought retains only what thought can claim by right."[23] Every society produces an image of thought, and the new image of thought never fully replaces the old image, but superposes the old one

19  Deleuze and Guattari, *A Thousand Plateaus,* 4.
20  Robert Porter, "From Clichés to Slogans: Towards a Deleuze-Guattarian Critique of Ideology," *Social Semiotics,* 20, no. 3 (2010): 233–45, at 239.
21  I am using Michel Pêcheux's expression "ideology-cloud" (*idéologie-nuage*) as discussed by Macherey, see *Le Sujet des normes,* 290–98. The other notion that Pêcheux introduced in his general theory of ideology in 1968 was "ideology-cement" (*idéologie-ciment*), which implies the proximity and materiality of ideology as opposed to the floating weightlessness of the "ideology-cloud."
22  Gilles Deleuze, *Difference and Repetition,* trans. Paul Patton (New York: Columbia University Press, 1994), xvii. Again in 1988, in an interview with François Ewald for *Le magazine littéraire,* Deleuze explains that noology should be the program of philosophy. See Deleuze, *Negotiations,* 148–49.
23  Gilles Deleuze and Félix Guattari, *What Is Philosophy?,* trans. Hugh Tomlinson and Graham Burchell (London/New York: Verso Books, 1994), 37.

as a new layer or stratum. Thus, Deleuze and Guattari refer to noological time as "a stratigraphic time":

A stratum or layer of the plane of immanence will necessarily be *above* or *below* in relation to another, and images of thought cannot arise in any order whatever because they involve changes of orientation that can be directly located only on the earlier image [...].[24]

Noologies do not arrive in sequence, the old one replacing the new one, rather, they accumulate over time; they are part of a process of sedimentation. Noology is the project of both diagnosing the current and the older strata (the images below), and constructing new layers of sedimentation. The production of new images of thought is particularly difficult and painful since it requires a certain violence to overcome the shared indifference attached to the activity of thinking.[25]

The new category of noology is necessary in their endeavor to leave behind the equivocation and the ambivalence attached to the notion of "ideology." I argue that it was not simply to rebut the Marxist tradition that both Foucault and Deleuze-Guattari adopted new terminologies: the organization of power or the "art of government" for Foucault, and noology for Deleuze and Guattari. This practice of using new terms (noology) to contribute to the re-elaboration of a classic concept (ideology) is not unique in Deleuze and Guattari. We can compare this to their treatment of the notion of "utopia," suggesting that it can be replaced by Samuel Butler's "Erewhon," a term that refers simultaneously to "No-where" and "Now-here."[26] Concepts are perishable and can be mutilated, they need to be re-activated

24  Ibid., 58.
25  I have attempted to explain this aspect of Deleuze's thought in Benoît Dillet, "What is Called Thinking? When Deleuze Walks Along Heideggerian Paths," *Deleuze Studies* 7, no. 2 (2013): 250–74.
26  "[I]n view of the mutilated meaning public opinion has given to it, perhaps utopia is not the best word" (Deleuze and Guattari, *What Is Philosophy?*, 100).

or remodeled to fit the new state of affairs. Just as Deleuze referred to Charles Péguy's expression that events can rot or decompose when losing their dynamism, concepts too can rot.[27] Every concept derives from a necessity but these are historically determined, and there is a historicity of concepts.

> We can admit indeed, given the conditions of formation, that "ideology" is not a very good concept [...] [but] are there concepts that can be considered "good all the way" and that did not need to be safeguarded against recuperations [*dérive*]?[28]

This effort of updating ideology-theory by Macherey should be welcome and pursued, hence my modest contribution to this debate here.

*Familialism*

When one is looking for ideology in *Anti-Oedipus,* "familialism" first comes to mind. Familialism could be defined as both the reduction by psychoanalysts of the forms of mental and social disorder to the Oedipal complex, as well as the strict naturalization of the family-structure that conditions this interpretative framework. Polemically, Deleuze and Guattari write about the Oedipal complex: "In reality it is a completely ideological beginning, for the sake of ideology."[29] For them, the Oedipal complex is not false, since such a position would be equally problematic and ideological, but *participates* in ideology ("for the sake of ideology"), and ultimately, in capital. The whole project of *Anti-Oedipus* was therefore "the denunciation of Oedipus as the "inevitable illusion" falsifying all historical production."[30] Their critique of ideology could not be clearer here. Yet we should not

27  Deleuze, *Negotiations,* 170.
28  Macherey, *Études,* 87.
29  Ibid., 101.
30  Gilles Deleuze, *Two Regimes of Madness,* ed. David Lapoujade, trans. Ames Hodges and Michael Taormina (Los Angeles: Semiotext(e), 2006), 309.

rush to the thought that the Oedipal schema is a falsifying production because it is repressing the individual, or because individuals desire it. This is the mistake that certain authors made by attempting to argue for a Freud-Marx synthesis. Reich and others were too quick at identifying "social repression [*répression*] and psychic repression [*refoulement*] at the cost of a series of illusions and led to hypostasize 'sexual liberation' as the object of the struggles of emancipation."[31] Contrary to these forms of Freudo-Marxism, Deleuze and Guattari treat familialism as an image of thought, and in doing so they will therefore argue that Oedipus does exist and, even more surprisingly, they will claim that the material existence of Oedipus is universal:

> Yes, Oedipus is universal. But the error lies in having believed in the following alternative: either Oedipus is the product of the social repression-psychic repression system, in which case it is not universal; or it is universal, and a position of desire. In reality, it is universal because it is the displacement of the limit that haunts all societies, the displaced represented [*le représenté déplacé*] that disfigures what all societies dread absolutely as their most profound negative: namely, the decoded flows of desire.[32]

In this remarkable passage, Deleuze and Guattari emphasize that the error of Oedipus will not disappear so easily given its material existence in society, particularly in relations with "universal history." But what is "universal history" and what is its relation to noology? Universal history should be understood as the contingent integration in all societies of two limits: the absolute limit of schizophrenia as the dazzling and anarchical creative production of the unconscious, and the relative limit of capital that is integrated within the social to produce its immanent dy-

---

31  Guillaume Sibertin-Blanc, *Deleuze et l'Anti-Œdipe: La production du désir* (Paris: Presses Universitaires de France, 2010), 82.

32  Deleuze and Guattari, *Anti-Oedipus,* 177.

namism.[33] Capitalism is ultimately hypocritical since it portrays itself as a moderate mechanism of distribution of wealth (via the notorious trickle down effect for instance) while functioning on the constant displacement of its limits: "things work well only providing they break down, crises [are] 'the means immanent to the capitalist mode of production.'"[34]

The overall objective of *Anti-Oedipus* is to show the correspondence and the analogy at work between familialism and capital. Capitalism can only constantly displace its limits by reintegrating new roles for "daddy-mommy-me."[35] In other words, the Oedipal noology is found not only at the level of psychoanalytic practice but, more crucially, at the level of the *socius*: it is the historical production of reality that is abstracted. Therefore, to study familialism noologically means to study its social institutions and its social (re)production, both in terms of content (related to bodies) and expressions (related to signs). Deleuze and Guattari want to "revamp the theory of ideology by saying that expressions and statements intervene directly in productivity, in the form of a production of meaning or sign-value."[36] Put differently, the only theory of ideology that they would agree with is one that studies the intervention of expressions and functions in the mode of libidinal and economic production. Such a general theory of ideology (as noology) would account for the images that create an adhesion to the capitalist system.

By taking a closer look at *Anti-Oedipus,* one finds this revamped theory of ideology beginning with what Deleuze and Guattari call the axiomatic. They refer to the capitalist axiomatic as the organization of rules (axioms) that underlie the capitalist

33  This thesis about the internal limit of capitalism that is constantly displaced is interpreted from Deleuze and Guattari's reading of Marx's *Capital* book III. They write: "If capitalism is the exterior limit of all societies, this is because capitalism for its part has no exterior limit, but only an interior limit that is capital itself and that it does not encounter, but reproduces by always displacing it" (Deleuze and Guattari, *Anti-Oedipus,* 230–31).

34  Ibid., 230.

35  Ibid., 51.

36  Deleuze and Guattari, *A Thousand Plateaus,* 89.

machinery, but this axiomatic is far from being static. On the contrary, it is extremely plastic and adaptable to new situations and forms of contestation: "How much flexibility there is in the axiomatic of capitalism, always ready to widen its own limits so as to add a new axiom to a previously saturated system!"[37] Deleuze and Guattari use the term axiomatic rather than ideology since it explains the operability of capitalism and the performativity of the capitalist axioms. The axiomatic constantly metamorphoses, or to be more precise, it is composed of layers of sedimentation, in which a new layer always covers a previous one. There is a constant movement forward, and the new axiom that supplements and modifies slightly the orientation of the capitalist axiomatic attempts to overshadow the previous axiom: "memory has become a bad thing."[38] The capitalist axiomatic has also emptied out the meaning of language and transformed it into a domain of "order-words":

> Above all, there is no longer any need of belief, and the capitalist is merely striking a pose when he bemoans the fact that nowadays no one believes in anything any more. Language no longer signifies something that must be believed, it indicates rather what is going to be done.[39]

Language is turned into a functional realm in which there is no room for enlarging sympathies. The axiomatic noologically intends to replace the social by the space and time of capital but "one must not think that it replaces the *socius*" since the social machine and the technical machines are two different types of machines.[40] In these extracts, Deleuze and Guattari conduct their ideology critique without falling prey to a cynicism that refuses to critique capitalism and its inner workings, but emphasize the disappearance of belief that underlies the capital-

37  Deleuze and Guattari, *Anti-Oedipus,* 238.
38  Ibid., 250.
39  Ibid.
40  Ibid., 251.

ist axiomatic. In short, while classical and orthodox Marxists argued that ideology distorted reality and led workers to forget about the material production of their lives, Deleuze and Guattari on the other hand demonstrate that ideology in the 1970s was characterized by the privation of those distorted realities (beliefs); ideology had become ideology-cement instead of ideology-cloud.[41]

Once all beliefs disappear, hope disappears, friendship and the family disappear, cynicism grows, and the social reproduction works through images that come to govern our existence. These images are the functions of thought that circulate in the *socius*:

> We have repudiated and lost all our beliefs that proceeded by way of objective representations. The earth is dead, the desert is growing: the old father is dead, the territorial father, and the son too, the despot Oedipus. We are alone with our bad conscience and our boredom, our life where nothing happens; nothing left but images that revolve within the infinite subjective representation. We will muster all our strength so as to believe in these images, from the depths of a structure that governs our relationships with them [...].[42]

This new economy of images appears in the ruins caused by cynicism and in the extreme faith in objectivity. Yet this objectivity is not sufficiently denounced, as Deleuze and Guattari note, for not being objective, but, on the contrary, for passing for objectivity. They critique the idea of general equivalence on which capitalism rests by demonstrating that "capitalists and their economists" assert that "surplus value cannot be determined mathematically."[43] The same capitalists do everything "in favor of the very thing they are bent on hiding: that it is not the

---

41  "The unidimensional society has taken away ideology's capacity to create illusions" (Macherey, *Le sujet des normes,* 324).

42  Deleuze and Guattari, *Anti-Oedipus,* 308.

43  Ibid., 228.

same money that goes into the pocket of the wage earner and is entered on the balance sheet of a commercial enterprise."[44] In this passage, Deleuze and Guattari present a concrete noological study, they uncover the institutionality and materiality of thought (the notorious "confidence of the market"). The institutional organization of the distribution of money that is supposedly rational and mathematic is in fact largely based on a dissimulation operated by the financial system: "one is correct in speaking of a profound *dissimulation* of the dualism of these two forms of money, payment and financing — the two aspects of banking practice."[45] In their noology critique, Deleuze and Guattari therefore find the hidden formula of the two forms of money that are mediated by the bank: ideology is located in the financial institutional system itself.[46] The paradox of money is that, on the one hand, we take money as being the most objective fact in our lives, but on the other, we know that it operates through "contingent rules" that are abstracted from our lives.[47]

To take an example, we can refer to the current "mediamacro" in place in the United Kingdom that equates government budgets with household budgets ("keeping the books") so that the ideological message of austerity "one should not spend more than one has" gets largely integrated into the *doxa*: everyone (individuals and firms) have to tighten their belts.[48] To equate indi-

44  Ibid.

45  Ibid., 229, emphasis in the original.

46  Read comments on Deleuze's distinction between an arithmetical and a differential understanding of surplus-value introduced in one of his Vincennes courses in December 1971: the first one is quantifiable while the second one refuses equivalence. The differential understanding emphasizes the construction of the equivalence between a unit of money and a unit of knowledge: "there is an encounter between a flow of money and a flow of knowledge" (Read, "Fetish is Always Actual," 91).

47  Martijn Konings, *The Emotional Logic of Capitalism: What Progressives Have Missed* (Stanford: Stanford University Press, 2015), 3.

48  I borrow the term "mediamacro" from Simon Wren-Lewis, to refer to the vulgarized discourse on macroeconomics largely present in the UK media. See Simon Wren-Lewis, "The Austerity Con," *London Review of Books* 37, no. 4, February 19, 2015, 9–11.

vidual household budgets and government budgets is extremely misleading and clearly participates in a political project.[49]

Yet, this apparent objectivity of capital, Deleuze and Guattari note, is "by no means a failure to recognize or an illusion of consciousness," but rather the productive essence of financial capitalism itself.[50] It is precisely because the desire for money is a desire for one's own powerlessness that the dissimulation is productive and not deceptive or distracting.[51] The difference between the absolute limit that schizophrenia represents (all structures break down in schizophrenia; it is a dissolution of the subject and productive work) and the relative limit of capitalism lies in the process of re-integrating the decoded flows of desire in an axiomatic.[52] As I explained earlier, the construction of this axiomatic is a constant process of adding new axioms, much like sedimentation: one function (axiom) does not fully replace the former function but only adds a new dimension to conjure and to push back the moment of the ultimate breakdown (the absolute limit). This is why "the bourgeois is justified in saying, not in terms of ideology, but in the very organization of his axiomatic: there is only one machine," and not two classes with opposing interests.[53] The notorious slogan of neoliberalism "there is no alternative" is not a mere ideological statement but an organization of the axiomatic, since the axiomatic is defined by its singularity that gathers all axioms and binds individuals into a single social machine. The "bourgeois" works at the noological level of functions and the axiomatic, that is in a post-ideological

49 This can be compared to Paul Krugman's oft-cited argument that business and economics should be differentiated. See Paul Krugman, "A Country Is Not a Company," *Harvard Business Review,* January–February 1996, 40–51.

50 Deleuze and Guattari, *Anti-Oedipus,* 239.

51 "[T]he flow of merchant capital's economic force and the flow that is derisively named 'purchasing power' — a flow made truly impotent [impuissanté] that represents the absolute impotence [impuissance] of the wage earner as well as the relative dependence of the industrial capitalist" (ibid., 238–39).

52 On this important distinction, see Deleuze and Guattari, *Anti-Oedipus,* 245–47.

53 Ibid., 254.

world making up the social machine. Once again Deleuze and Guattari want to contrast an analysis that takes into account noology, functions, and the axiomatic on the one hand, with the ill-suited dogmatic Marxist framework that focuses on class consciousness, false consciousness, thought-contents, beliefs, and the "superstructure" on the other. It is precisely because beliefs and ideology have vanished that the Marxist ideology theory (although Deleuze and Guattari portray a rather crude version of it) is no longer relevant.

## Images of capital and images of images

Having discussed how Deleuze and Guattari transformed the project of ideology critique into a project that takes into account desire, not as an immaterial and weightless substance but in its materiality, we can now go as far as to conclude that they aimed to study the material inscriptions of ideology: transforming ideology critique into geology or physics.[54] At this point, we need to come back to the loss of belief and the reign of images to understand how Deleuze provides an answer to questions about the capitalist exploitation of abstract desire in *Cinema 2: The Time-Image.*

There are at least two reasons why the turn to images is crucial here. First, instead of representation it is the materiality of images that interests Deleuze, the circulation of these images, continuing in a way Benjamin's early reflections on the reproducibility of images. Second, the analyses of images continue the noology project, of studying the historicity of the images of thought.

Social reproduction is established with image-functions, and just as philosophy has conceptual personae, capitalism has "figures." Through the production of these figures and roles es-

---

54 "But in reality, the unconscious belongs to the realm of physics; the body without organs and its intensities are not metaphors, but matter itself" (Deleuze and Guattari, *Anti-Oedipus,* 283).

tablished within the axiomatic, individuals become functions integrated in the axiomatic:

> [Individuals] are nothing more or less than configurations or images produced by the points-signs, the breaks-flows, the pure "figures" of capitalism: the capitalist as personified capital — i.e., as a function derived from the flow of capital; and the worker as personified labor capacity — i.e., a function derived from the flow of labor.[55]

Deleuze and Guattari conclude that, through the mechanism of social reproduction in place in familialism, private persons are secondary, they are "images of images," images of the second order.[56] The familialist images operate by copying the images of capital. This is why they call these private images, "images of images" or "simulacra."[57] In capitalism the images of the first order are generated to capture the flows of desire by capital. Desires are captured and abstracted to fit in one of the images produced by capitalism: "[C]apitalism fills its field of immanence with images: even destitution, despair, revolt — and on the other side, the violence and the oppression of capital — become images of destitutions, despair, revolt, violence, or oppression."[58] It is also because of the withering of belief that the old understanding of ideology as belief system does not work anymore for neoliberal societies (after the 1970s). Beliefs have been "flattened" by the axiomatic, to use a word that is recurrent in this third chapter of *Anti-Oedipus*. An entire "psychology of the priest" is organized by the images of capital that are reproduced by their simulacra in the family structure (the father as the capitalist, and so on).[59] But contrary to what we may think at first, there is no contra-

---

55  Deleuze and Guattari, *Anti-Oedipus,* 264.

56  Ibid.

57  Ibid.

58  Ibid.

59  "Father, mother, and child thus become the simulacrum of the images of capital ("Mister Capital, Madame Earth," and their child the Worker), with the result that these images are no longer recognized at all in the desire

diction between the withering of belief and the extreme moralization of society.[60] Bad conscience is socially organized and reinforced by the images and the melodrama. In the economy of images, the bad passions are strictly dominating:

> [D]epression and guilt [are] used as a means of contagion, the kiss of the Vampire: aren't you ashamed to be happy? follow my example, I won't let you go before you say, "It's my fault." O ignoble contagion of the depressives, neurosis as the only illness consisting in making others ill […] the abject desire to be loved, the whimpering at not being loved enough, at not being "understood" […].[61]

In the vacuity of belief and the reign of images, the role of schizoanalysis in *Anti-Oedipus* and of cinema in *Cinema 2: The Time-Image,* would be to produce images against the images of capital. The struggle against the economy of sad passions cannot be launched at the level of positive messages and content, but rather at the material level, in the physics of thought, to change the image of thought (what it means to think): "[I]mages are not in our head, in our brain. The brain is just one image among others."[62] It is an image of thought to conceive the brain as a recipient of images, while in fact the organization of the brain is co-constituted with the exteriorizations. The image of the brain shapes how thought processes take place, what limitations one puts on one's thought. Deleuze would argue that the powers that be have an interest in keeping a socially accepted image of the brain as a calculating machine that fits the *homo economicus.* Noology critique operates from inventing new human and non-human assemblages instead of clinging to old structures of thought. There is no contradiction between the micro and

that is determined to invest only their simulacrum. The familial determinations become the application of the social axiomatic" (ibid.)

60 On this paradox, see Mark Alizart, *Pop théologie: protestantisme et postmodernité* (Paris: Presses Universitaire de France, 2015).

61 Ibid., 268–69.

62 Deleuze, *Negotiations,* 42, translation modified.

macro levels, instead the flattened understanding of ideology takes into account the relations between all levels. "It is not that our thinking starts from what we know about the brain but that any new thought traces uncharted channels directly through its matter, twisting, folding and fissuring it."[63] Thinking is a microphysical operation in the brain, rather than an immaterial product. But this microphysics does not mean that noology forgets about the hierarchization and verticalization at work in societies — familialism and hylemorphism are examples of such relations of domination.

What is fundamental in noology critique is that it does not and cannot work without inventing new forms of thought. The production of new images in cinema is an example of such a production for Deleuze to "restore our belief in this world."[64] Deleuze distinguishes here between a cerebral cinema and a cinema of control.[65] While the latter produces clichés and melodramas, the former creates new types of images (through lectosigns and noosigns) in the chain of images. What interests Deleuze in cinema is how certain images attempt to break from clichés (or the "images of images") that private individuals are subjected to in the capitalist axiomatic. Since we are embedded in the dark world of images of images (simulacra), we can only rework these types of images by standing behind the camera, from the depth of the cave, instead of succumbing to these:

On the one hand, the image constantly sinks to the state of cliché [...] [and] it is a civilization of the cliché where all the powers have an interest in hiding images from us [...]. On the other hand, at the same time, the image constantly attempts to break through the cliché, to get out of the cliché.[66]

63  Ibid., 149.
64  Gilles Deleuze, *Cinema 2: The Time-Image,* trans. Hugh Tomlinson and Robert Galeta (Minneapolis: University of Minnesota Press, 1989), 172.
65  This is particularly well contrasted in his letter to Serge Daney (Deleuze, *Negotiations,* 68–79).
66  Deleuze, *Cinema 2,* 21.

The project of creating "images" — and therefore brains ("give me a brain"[67]) — in cinema allows for the possibility of breaking with the civilization of clichés in order to believe in this world again.

67  Ibid., 196.

# 7

# Passion, Cinema,
# and the Old Materialism

*Louis-Georges Schwartz*

At the end of the twentieth century, cinema underwent regime change, not death. Cinema has become universalized in the form of gently used media. Its leading edge subordinates both movement and image to hostility, and articulates affect through a new set of images and signs. In the past, cinematic affect was transindividual, molecular, and social; the new regime expresses affect as a molar ready made imposed on individuals by the economy. The films themselves make it clear that these changes erupted from recent capitalist restructuring of both production and the markets. As a method for understanding the interaction of cinema and capital, I will force Gilles Deleuze's *Cinema 1* and *Cinema 2* to become a draft, a draft of his lost project *Grandeur de Marx* and analyze affect in today's image regime with Alex Rivera's *Sleep Dealer* (2008).

In *Cinema 1* and *Cinema 2,* Deleuze describes a passionate art that narrates a consciousness which must either suffer the world or change it. If consciousness cannot recreate the world according to its desires, the world as it is degrades and confuses consciousness while weakening bodies. Under each regime, the labor-capital relation determines labor's capacity to act. The movement-image presents an active consciousness moving rationally through a comprehensible world to solve problems, accomplish goals, and execute programs. The time-image, on the other hand, presents a passional consciousness, stunned by the world situation, and looking for the determinations of its circumstances. Deleuze's two cinematic regimes irrupt dialectically from the levels of subsumption before and after World War II. The third period is determined by the non-relation between surplus populations and surplus capital in our time. Real subsumption was a fact of labor's life but workers' victories were in struggles over absolute surplus value, the length of work, not its intensity. The prewar movement-image developed during an era dominated by struggles in the capitalist core over the formal subsumption of labor: over the length of the working day and the right to vacations and holidays. The movement-image lost salience, and the time-image replaced it once Taylorization had been completed and introduced even in semi-peripheral countries such as Italy. It expresses the real subsumption of labor, in which capital controls every aspect of the labor process and workers struggle over hourly wages and working conditions. With the twenty-first century comes Cinema Hostis and full subsumption, in which the difference between labor and being available for labor becomes increasingly indiscernible: every aspect of social reproduction has been included in capital's circuits of exchange. The ever rising organic composition of capital — the ratio of machine work to human labor — leads to structural unemployment, relative surplus population that cannot be absorbed into the waged labor force, and a working class seeking to abolish itself.

Each cinematic period expresses affect through its own signs within the mood appropriate to the exigencies of the economic situation from which the regimes spring. The cinematic regimes not only have specific affective signs; between the three periods, the forms of affective expression change. The movement-image suffers the world with anxiety. Its differentiated affects crystalize in subjects who are necessary to the disciplined movements entailed in the production and circulation of commodities. Within the passionate boredom of the time-image, subjects have themselves become commodities which encounter affects externally in whatever-spaces that are abstracted by the pure sensation of time passing. Cinema Hostis's mood of enmity can only repeat itself in the form of weaponized affects used by parties to a struggle.

Economy has lain waste to the world and exterminated every form of life opposing production and exchange. Economy creates subjects with interests which it sets to work against one another and has only ever been an organization of hostility. The emergence of enmity in cinema can be verified by consulting various recent dossiers on contemporary film such as *Neoliberalism and Global Cinema,* edited by Jyotsna Kapur and Keith Wagner. The articles in that collection describe "ghostly landscapes filled with wandering souls and the scattered body parts of shattered dreams, suppressed rage, disappointments, and despair,"[1] a poetics of

> [t]he violence of things over the living, of the lifelong dependence on debt, of mannequin bodies that real people aspire for, and finally the power of money to control not only the quality of life, but the right to life itself [...].[2]

They find a cinema that links the hospital "character attitudes" to "architectures of urban space" in order to map "the destabilizing of community in an age of survivalist capitalism."[3]

---

1 Xudong Zang, "Market Socialism and Its Discontent: Jia Zhangke's Cinematic Narrative of China's Transition in the Age of Global Capital," in *Neoliberalism and Global Cinema: Capital, Culture and Marxist Critique,* eds. Jyotsna Kapur and Keith B. Wagner, 135–65 (London: Routledge, 2011), 137.

2 Jyotsna Kapur, "The Underdevelopment of Development: Neoliberalism and the Crisis of Bourgeois Individualism," in *Neoliberalism and Global Cinema: Capital, Culture and Marxist Critique,* eds. Jyotsna Kapur and Keith B. Wagner, 197–216 (London: Routledge, 2011), 198.

3 Keith B. Wagner, "Fragments of Labor: Neoliberal Attitudes and Architectures in Contemporary South Korean Cinema," in *Neoliberalism and Global Cinema: Capital, Culture and Marxist Critique,* eds. Jyotsna Kapur and Keith B. Wagner, 217–38 (London: Routledge, 2011), 218.

Perhaps to bring cinema's recent hostile mood out most clearly, one only needs to recollect the quizzical looks on Parisian's faces when the participants in *Chronique d'un été* (Edgar Morin and Jean Rouch, 1961) asked them whether they were happy. In 1959, it seemed an absurd question, a question out of synch with the film's abstracted spaces and circulating subjects. The out of joint question created a fractured horizon keeping *Chronique d'un été*'s concrete durations from harmonizing, allowing the film to depict the cracks of the past between the cobblestones over which the characters walk, as well as the shadows of intensified struggle to come. Today one cannot imagine anything but the most soiled clichés of Sarkozy administration's "happiness index" from a film organized around that question.

According to Deleuze, in the movement-image, affects well up after movements of perception, waves of sound and light, have flowed from a world to a subject. Affect appears when that movement, temporarily enclosed in the subject, and no longer a motion between points A and B, becomes a twinge of pure quality. Affect eventually further sublimates into thought or flows out to the world. Although the movement-image's affects crystalize within subjects, they result from a-human and transpersonal movements initiated outside that subject. Affects individuate themselves inside the sensory motor arc linking perception, a center of indetermination and the incurved horizon of the world. In the movement-image affects express themselves on subjects' surfaces, on their faces, resulting in what Deleuze calls the affection-image. The affection-image has a sign of composition, the facial close up, and a genetic sign, the any-space-whatever.

The regime of the movement-image expresses the chronotopes of an era during which surplus value extraction rates were high enough for labor to constitute itself as a subject capable of executing a program. Movement-images depict the form of time needed by the working class in order to revolutionize its struggle over the length of the working day. In an essay entitled "Three Temporal Dimensions of Class Struggle," George Caffentzis elaborates on the two forms of time proper to capital: the linear time used to measure production and the circular time used to track the reproduction of capital.[4] Both forms measure movement. When labor appears as part of capital, it too must rely on those forms of temporality. Gilles Dauvé and Karl Nesic's description of this period as "programmatist"[5] implies that labor needed forms of time that measure the movements of production: a circular time to orient itself within the capital's expanded reproduction, and a linear time to articulate its programs. In this period labor needed a temporality capable of linking perception to moving bodies, functioning as centers of indetermination and subjectivity, a temporality within which the actions of those bodies could meet their objects in the world. If the production process determines the essence of the labor-capital relation it does so by determining the time of social relations.

In the facial close up, affect appears as a mobile impulse on a sensory nerve. The facial close up composes affects from the relations between facial features and distributes those affects along a spectrum between the active pole of desire and the reflective pole of wonder. The tight framing of the close up abstracts the face from its spatiotemporal coordinates, allowing films to express pure qualities independently of situations within which qualities are realized. A face with features that break its outline expresses the extreme of desire while a stilled, plate-like face expresses wonder. Writing about this period of formal subsumption, Jason Read shows that capital creates a mode of subjectivity immanent to the abstract labor power that it produces.[6] Individual, "free," skilled, servile workers and cooperating subjects born of industry were both results of the contradictory movement of capital's antagonisms, and its distribution of a range of affects between subjects.

4   George Caffentzis, *In Letters of Blood and Fire: Work, Machines, and the Crisis of Capitalism* (Oakland: PM Press, 2013), 82–87.

5   Gilles Dauvé and Karl Nesic, "Love of Labour? Love of Labour Lost…," *End Notes 1* (2008): 104–52.

6   Jason Read, *The Micro-Politics of Capital: Marx and the Prehistory of the Present* (New York: SUNY Press, 2003), 62.

Charlie Chaplin's *Modern Times* (1936) exemplifies affection-image compositions in the movement-image regime. Chaplin's Tramp character goes from factory to prison to home, mechanically stumbling upon one enclosed space after another. Chaplin's comedy comes from responding to situations with inappropriate movements, including the micro-movements of his face, thus transforming the situation in unexpected ways. Despite the relatively low number of close ups in *Modern Times,* the Tramp's face remains disconnected from the space around it, separated by its different make up and the abnormal connection between his expression and the actions. By crystallizing the "wrong affect" the Tramp space makes the determinations of other characters' expressions intelligible. He makes the audience wait to see how he will escape the difficulties each presents to him, suspending the laughter in the passionate element of anxiety.

The Tramp's face moves inappropriately. When the lunch signal sounds while he tries to rescue a fellow worker trapped in the gears of a huge machine, the Tramp gets his colleague's food, eats, and feeds the other worker with a calm and beatific expression of enjoyment rather than the expected resolved or panicked look. When the Tramp accidentally inhales some cocaine hidden in a saltshaker while in jail, his face is a spasm of desire, unlike the faces of the other prisoners and the guards, who do not know the reason for his over-stimulation. Perceiving the factory, the jail, and the home overwhelms the Tramp, and an affect uncorrelated with his situation wells up in him. The Tramp's irrational affect exposes the process of industrial subjectification, and eventually forges a way out.

In the film's conclusion, the Tramp and his lover find themselves excluded from all enclosures, homeless, and unemployed, abandoned on the side of the road. In a close medium shot their two faces pass through series of expressions from surrender to determination in an accelerated coda of facial expressions. The lovers' faces finally become smiling masks expressing their newly found power to take the road out of the metropolis toward the abstracted horizon of the industrial us's mythical road.

As Read's work demonstrates, subsumption's affects emerge from the latent possibilities in the flows and axioms specific to that period of capitalism as opposed to new affects capable of transforming the image regime within which they function. Nonetheless potential for the new emerges in the affection-image's genetic sign.

Deleuze points out that close-ups sometimes include a fragment of space to the side of the face, removed from its spatio-temporal coordinates. Any space can be framed as a provisionally closed set of relations, just as the face can.[7] Such abstracted whatever-spaces function as the affection-image's genetic sign, causing semiotic mutations and articulating a different image regime. Subjects disappear in whatever-spaces, and affect appears externally as an abstracted set of relations enduring a passage of time. The time-image emerges as the increased use of whatever-spaces changes cinematic affect from an expression crystalized within a subject into the time of relations in general, opening it to non-human qualities, and further sublating affect into powers of thought.

The second cinematic regime, the time-image, expresses the period of real subsumption after World War II, when Taylorization had been completed in the core and older industries in which the work had not been automated and made technical had been bombed out of existence and rebuilt. Capital now possessed and controlled the techniques of labor as well as its forms, and workers sought to escape the plane of capital rather than transforming it from within. Instead of measuring movements internal to capitalism, the time-image rendered time in a pure state.

The massive and uneven destruction of capital in the Second World War led to a shift in the labor capital relation, which caused the movement-image to lose salience in the capitalist semi-periphery during a new round of primitive accumula-

7   Gilles Deleuze, *Cinema 1: The Movement-Image,* trans. Hugh Tomlinson and Barbara Habberjam (Minneapolis: University of Minnesota Press, 1986), 108.

tion. This phase, in which the bourgeoisie takes what it needs for capitalism to function by any means necessary, formed the base from which modern cinema erupted. Italy provides a clear example of this process, which explains much about its postwar cinema and perhaps also explains the Italian fascination with phrases such as "consumer capitalism," "social reproduction," "biopower," "biopolitics," and "the social factory." When the cycle of restructuring initiated by postwar primitive accumulation ended, and the factories started to shrink, Italian insurrectionists still believed the revolutionary mass must be composed of productive laborers, and so they decided that exchange and reproduction must produce somehow surplus value, even if such a supposition was questionable.

After the war, the modernization of Italian agriculture drove peasants from the south into vast, ghettoized labor pools in the *brogate,* or peripheral slums, of northern cities. This migration spewed out immigrants who became Australians or, like Antonio Berruti, minor characters in the Paris of films such as *Breathless* (Jean-Luc Godard, 1960). Modernizing agriculture meant that many fewer laborers were required to grow the same amount of produce and livestock; the resulting migration to industrial centers transformed Italian peasantry into a proletariat with a massive unemployed layer. "Between 1950 and 1967, [...] more than a third of the Italian population moved from one district to another."[8] The proletarianized reserve labor pools were forced to work to live, yet capital did not require all of their labor. In capitalism reserve labor pools must provide for their own continued existence because capitalism deprives potential workers of the means of reproduction in order to force them to be available as laborers — the definition of proletarianization. In the abode of production the real subsumption of labor accelerated with the Marshall Plan that fueled Italian hyper-development. Pier Paolo Pasolini would remark that he saw the assembly line implanted throughout Italy in a ten-year period.

8   Ernest Dowson, "The Italian Background," *Radical America* 7, no. 2 (1973): 7–14, at 8.

Every aspect of proletariat's existence was now determined and regulated by capital. Labor began to realize that only by "leaving the plan(e) of capital, and never ceasing to leave it," "a mass becomes increasingly revolutionary and destroys the dominant equilibrium [...]."[9]

In the time-image, characters attempt to find a way off the planes subsuming them by thinking the determinants of the situations that trap them. The stunned characters cannot react to incoming movements effectively and float on the forces that determine them. They become perceivers, or what Deleuze calls "spiritual automata,"[10] instead of agents. Rendered semi-catatonic by the banal intolerability of the post-war world, these perceivers see far but are only capable of small acts. The seers must find a subtle way to reconnect with the world, just as labor had to find a way to sustain itself where capital had alienated it from all means of production. The determinations of the time-image's situations offer a way out, a potential for autonomy.

Once cybernetics' controlling networks had replaced the disciplinary enclosures of formal subsumption, full subsumption, became possible in the capitalist core. Once economy engulfed all bodies and minds, creating a networked subjectification, characters began to rely on the structure of the market the way we depend on the physical laws to move through space.

> The members of society are thus violently isolated, "individualized," subjected to personalized (and hence inquisitive) abstract measurements that appear natural (or scientific) or appear to be the intrinsic property of "progressive" technical systems (or the technical objects of those systems). If persons are thingified, transformed into simple elements of account-

9  Gilles Deleuze and Félix Guattari, *A Thousand Plateaus: Capitalism And Schizophrenia,* trans. Brian Massumi (Minneapolis: University of Minnesota Press, 1987), 472.

10  Gilles Deleuze, *Cinema 2: The Time Image,* trans. Hugh Tomlinson and Robert Galeta (Minneapolis, University of Minnesota Press, 1989), 169–70.

ing, technical things (or commodities) become, conversely, not just alive but dominating.[11]

As Read points out, under real subsumption the very affect of labor belongs to capital.[12] The restructuring of capital means changes in its flows of people, changes in the axioms that determine subjects and social relations. Capital increasingly disguised the capitalist relation itself, appropriating all formal and embodied human knowledge to its own appearance as something inherently productive, while making labor appear as redundancy. The omnipotence of capital bored us; it left us with nothing to do but withdraw ourselves. The time-image expresses real subsumption as an almost empty, subtractive cinema that makes the processes of capture, of abstraction, and domination perceivable, revealing a political order born of the power of economy and its categorizations — one that reduces human action to labor and relative surplus populations to bare life.

The cuts marking off the whatever-spaces that endure the time-images affects separate rather than connect shots. The characters in the films are too overwhelmed to become subjects and the affects refer to collective bodies that are ripped away from themselves and their worlds. Like the serial edits, bodies in the time-image assert their presence separately from the subjectivities connected to them or the space around them; they occupy an isolated space interrupting the image often enclosing away from other, normal bodies.

In Roberto Rossellini's *Europa '51,* Irene perceives the Roman slums as indifferent spaces, the abstraction of the streets and interiors standing into contrast with the cartographic specificity of the bourgeois home. In her family, she works as a redundant housewife with a waged staff who she manages instead of doing domestic labor directly. The unwaged existence of the poor

11 Jacques Fradin, *Economy, Ecumenes, Communism: Economy as the Devastation of Ecumenes, Communism as Exit from Economy,* trans. Robert Hurley (*No New Ideas,* n.d.), 20, http://no-new-ideas-press.tumblr.com/post/126683784621/economy-is-constituted-and-develops-through-the

12 Read, *The Micro-Politics of Capital,* 2.

and destitute women marks *Europa '51*'s Rome as a space of bare life, the mode of human beings unable to sustain citizenship: the formless being. Irene's mother mentions bare life's essential figure when she warns her daughter that communists will end up in concentration camps if war breaks out again. Irene sees the factory she visits as the yard for a camp, haunting the edges of the film with the figure. Giorgio Agamben points out that since World War II camps have become the *nomos* of the modern metropolis, figuring the transformation of political space into zones of force.[13] Variations on camp space, whatever-spaces, separate themselves from any world. Women enclosed within the forced labor of private reproduction incarnate bare life in societies of control, a status that paradoxically confers on their potential refusal of that labor, the power to end the reproduction of capitalism.

Through the banal, bored subjectivity of a stunned housewife, *Europa '51* expresses a revolutionary desire: the desire to see the world just as it is in order to destroy its mediations. Irene's desire surges within the difference between a zone marked as expressing the actual contradictions of social reproduction in post-war Italy, her home, and a fantastical zone presented as a virtual alternative mode of reproduction, the slums. The film presents both spaces through Irene's schematic, time-imaged perceptions. Her refusal of her family's private reproduction of the bourgeoisie and her flight into collectivized proletarian social reproduction functions are not simply expressions of a desire to perform women's work by other means. They are impressions of an impersonal need for systemic change based on a change in her society's mode of reproduction.

Control and society both come to an end with the emergence of full subsumption. Under full subsumption, the organic composition of capital has risen to a point where capital cannot extract enough surplus value from labor to keep growing. It must start distributing extant value upwards by commodifying every

---

13  Giorgio Agamben, *Homo Sacer: Sovereign Power and Bare Life,* trans. Daniel Heller-Roazen (Stanford: Stanford University Press, 1998), 166–88.

aspect of human existence and subjecting us to universalized exchange. Simultaneously capital accumulates wealth by dispossession through legal or military force, which is the contemporary form of primitive accumulation. In this phase, capital governs by abandonment. An asocial formation arises between numb bodies governed by a destituent power and unmediated violence.[14] The penetration of economy into every aspect of life is more than legible in the HSBC Holdings advertisement reading "in the future, there will be no more markets waiting to emerge." When living becomes indiscernible from exchange, nothing new will emerge. Various all too familiar features of the contemporary economy have transformed what little time workers could use for their reproduction into time during which they must be available for work.[15] Concretely this means: last-minute scheduling practices in minimum wage jobs, the tendency toward independent contracting in higher waged sectors, the growth of the flat corporation, the use of communications technology to tether us to our bosses, etc. Meanwhile, the "universal market" in services has completely colonized the sphere of reproduction. In the period of empire, life is completely subordinated to the economy and movement and time to hostility. For Tiqqun, the Hostis names that which has taken the place of social relations at a certain moment of the moving contradiction — the lived economy that reduces us to bare life. The cinematic expression of this contradiction results in films in which each is the enemy of each and the camera is the enemy of all.

The prehistory of Cinema Hostis includes the development of a specific form of reality television in which characters live together while being constantly recorded. As initially developed by PBS's *An American Family* (1971), in reality television hostility sometimes breaks out between the characters and at other times between the characters and the intrusive recording apparatus.

14 Giorgio Agamben, "For a Theory of Destituent Power: Public Lecture in Athens," November 16, 2013, http://www.chronosmag.eu/index.php/g-agamben-for-a-theory-of-destituent-power.html.
15 Jonathan Crary, *24/7: Late Capitalism and the Ends of Sleep* (London and New York: Verso, 2013).

This form originates along with the crisis that brings capitalism's golden age to a close. It comes at the very moment when the final distinct elements of reproduction start to merge with the universal market as capital restructures, intensifying circulation in order to compensate for flat growth in production.

Starting around 1989, declining rates of surplus value and the development of circuits of exhibition and exchange, such as VHS and cable, from which copyright owners could profit, fueled labor strife over residuals between actors and writers, and studios. Labor strife then drove the development of diverse forms of reality television, a format that can do without either writers or actors. As the annual global mass of surplus value declined, the shows stimulated hostility between the charters by making them compete to see who will be last to be excluded from the living arrangement as well as between the charters and the camera, intensifying and thematically presenting hostility in the capitalist ideological form of "competition."

Rivera's *Sleep Dealer* develops the affective signs of the Hostis while mapping full subsumption from the perspective of the surplus populations it generates due to the high organic composition of capital. Full subsumption separates the proletariat from itself as flows of people increasingly swerve away from flows of money for which they compete.

In Rivera's film, Memo leaves his native Oaxacan farming village, which has been desiccated by a dam that privatized its water source. He goes to find work in a *maquinaria* in a border city, where the laborers remote operate construction robots in the US. *Sleep Dealer* develops the rift while mapping full subsumption from the perspective of the surplus populations generated by the contemporary economy. Full subsumption means a high degree of automation, which means fewer waged workers and larger relative surplus populations. In addition to marginal profit from exchange, capital relies on dispossession as form of accumulation. The current hedge-fund driven land grab in Africa illustrates the point. It is there that populations are driven off land that will be farmed mechanically, but they will never be absorbed into the economy, because industry has also been mechanized. Paradoxically, full subsumption means that as capital integrates labor more completely, separations within the proletariat intensify as capital swerves its monetary flows away from people.

The new restructuring of capitalist flows requires new axioms that produce new types and forms of subjectivity. In Cinema Hostis, affective rift is the degree zero image from which others differentiate themselves. A rift sets up an antagonism between characters defined exclusively in terms of their separation from each other, and over the course of a film, the camera takes up all the positions within the antagonism. *Sleep Dealer* doesn't exactly set up an antagonism between two class subjects. Instead it sets up a complex antagonism among the workers themselves by using commodification to create a separation in the most intimate relationship in the film, that between Memo and his lover Luz. Although they seem in love, she sells her memories of being with him on an internet market. When Memo finds out that she sells her memories of him, their relationship swerves because a commodity is made for the purposes of selling. Memo can no longer read Luz's intent in seeing him as a form of affection or attraction. It becomes a form of economy. Although the film establishes the possibility that workers can bond together as workers in the very beginning, the film divides those characters in an extreme way before uniting them in a palpably false manner.

Cinematic rifts create a field of relations between bodies from a specified position within a totality of asocial relations. The rift's signs of composition form a spectrum between the pole of visors and the pole of frones. Visors render percepts of living bodies from positions in an antagonistic field of economic relations, while frones render a technical image surveying that field. The part of the spectrum closer to frones allows commercial films to use another recording device within the diegesis as an alibi for a film's own enunciative hostility toward its characters. The various hybrid visor-drone (hand held) cameras in the *Blair Witch Project* and *Paranormal Activity* function as a specification of hostile camera separate from the base level of enunciation. Although a drone has a palpably technical essence that can be combined with a visor's organic character, it does not form part of a neuro-image[16] or an interactive-image.[17] The drone's image appears on the screens of the devices that keep us available for labor and turn all space and time into a potentially laborious chronotope mediating the economization of the social reflected in the Cinema Hostis.

Luz's traffic in her memories of being with Memo allows Rivera to develop the rift in effort to allegorize different levels of the materiality of labor. Luz sells her memory on a network she plugs into through nodes on her body of the same kind as the nodes through which Memo controls the construction robots when he sells his labor time. A US military drone pilot who shot Memo's father buys Luz's subjective and semi-subjective shots from her perspective. Memo, Luz, and the pilot structurally belong to a decomposed class and the interests of each contradict the interests of another. *Sleep Dealer* brings them together through the very commodity markets separating them. The pilot buys Luz's memories to find Memo, and eventually helps him to destroy the dam that has privatized the water in Memo's region, turning the farmers of his village into a surplus population. The film hastens to its close with Memo helping the pilot disappear.

In sum: Cinema Hostis's first image-type, the rift, has two signs of composition: visors, shots from the point of view of a human enemy, and drones or lens genetic sign, a shot from the point of view of a diegetically displayed camera. *Sleep Dealer* combines visors with drones by having Luz sell her memories. She becomes both a human enemy and a hostile recording device. The clinamen is the rift's genetic sign. A clinamen combines multiple, antagonistic points of view in a single extended take, establishing each perspective through a reframing.

16  Patricia Pisters, *The Neuro-Image: A Deleuzian Film-Philosophy of Digital Screen Culture* (Stanford: Stanford University Press, 2012).
17  Kristen Daly, "Cinema 3.0: The Interactive-Image." *Cinema Journal* 50, no. 1 (2010): 81–98.

# 8

# Death of Deleuze,
# Birth of Passion

*David U.B. Liu*

Fig. 1. Detail from the predella from the altarpiece of the Crucifixion by Cornelis Engebrechtsz, ca. 1515–20, Lakenhal Museum in Leiden. Author's photograph, used with kind permission of the Lakenhal Museum.

I begin with the most familiar haiku of Bashō:

古池や
蛙飛び込む
水の音。

*Furuike ya*
*Kahadzu (kawazu) tobikomu*
*Mizu no oto.*

At the olden pond,
A frog (of yore) jumps right in.
The sound of water.[1]

The sound of water. What's it like? Is it a wee blip in the stillness of the old, jaded pond? Or is it a triumphal plop that shatters the slumbering silence? What affect unfolds here? Is it the frog that jitters to the onslaught of the cold mass of water while shot putting itself over the pond and flails? Or is it the unwilling water that parts passionally, suffering, to make room for this unruly intruder? Who is undergoing whom, how, how long — there and *here in the pond of our mind*?

On November 4, 1995, another frog jumped: Gilles Deleuze, famous philosopher, lifetime professor, family man — sick man for all his adult life.[2] He did not jump, however, into an idyllic, shy pool of mucky green water, but (clap!) smashingly into pavement. His launching pad was not one of placid lily or firm ground, but a window. So let us start here, right on that windowsill. The French press reported Deleuze's suicide as a *défenestration* — "jumping out of a window" — thus expressing an unwindowing, a sort of unframing. *Il s'est défenestré*, he jumped out of a window, he unwindowed, unframed himself. The language, still shaking from its own jolts and jumps, declares that suicide by leaping out a window was not only common within the modern urban architectural context of the country, of the Paris of its modern architect Georges-Eugène Haussmann, but also recognized distinctly in the typology of that "deadly sin" against the form of the society or state made lesser by it. Accordingly,

1   Transliteration and translation are mine; the word in parentheses being the modern pronunciation of *kahadzu* (frog).

2   Black humor and irony aside, my use of the image of the leap is also an allusion — and in homage — to Deleuze's own idea (with coauthor Félix Guattari) of various instantiations of the "leap" (*saut*) operative in art (from chaos to the composition), science (with bound feet onto calculus) and philosophy (across the fissure of hate and coexistent chaos among concepts). See Gilles Deleuze and Félix Guattari, *What Is Philosophy?*, trans. Hugh Tomlinson and Graham Burchell (London and New York: Verso, 1994), 203.

it seems to imply too that those who leap out of windows are foreclosing on themselves the "fenestral" openness to life — as sanctioned and drawn by the state political economy (cf. the iconic man jumping out of the North Tower of the World Trade Center on 9/11/01). To this anon will we return. One thinks of Émile Durkheim's famous *fin-de-siècle* study on suicide as a sign of *anomie* or general passional disorder.[3]

The death of Deleuze is no easy topic — nor should it be. Even at the level of linguistic description, we are at a loss. In English we would say: "he killed himself." But in the French press the same event is not given as "il s'est tué" ("he killed himself") but "il s'est donné la mort": "He gave himself (or was given) death." Is it a matter of giving death or taking away life, of donation or abreption? This is a tight conundrum, and scholars have done none too well with it. On the one hand, few scholars of this philosopher have chosen to discuss it at all. It is as though most thought it improper or embarrassing to slump to the low filth of biography — particularly an awkward one, when all that should count is the thought, the concept, the brilliant *Nachlaß* or *Nachklang* (not *impact,* please) of his works! Mind over body, I guess. Worse, they may have considered it scholarly suicide to be promoting the star of this philosopher of life — with however much *nuance* and *finesse,* when he himself seems to have chosen an abrupt, "unforced" death,[4] maybe not quite unthinkingly, but desperately. It is too glaring of a contradiction (and blaring distraction), as it seems Deleuze's death gives too much fodder to those bent on defaming any post-Nietzschean thought as just godless, "posty" nihilism. Or is this silence merely the old

3  Émile Durkheim, *Suicide: A Study in Sociology,* trans. John A. Spaulding and George Simpson (New York: The Free Press, 1997 (original 1897)).

4  I say "seems" because in at least one reading of Baruch Spinoza's treatment of suicide (Baruch Spinoza, *Ethics,* trans. Edwin Curley [London: Penguin Classics, 1996], IV.P20s), Spinoza appears to characterize the causes of suicide as being external, thus taking away internal agency from the suicide. See Jason E. Smith, "A Taste for Life (On Some Suicides in Deleuze and Spinoza)," *Parrhesia* 10 (2010): 75–85, esp. 78–79, http://www.parrhesia-journal.org/parrhesia10/parrhesia10_smith.pdf. Further discussion below.

Kantian reserve erecting its own quiet wall between the public and private acts and utterances of a "dyophysite" citizen-philosopher?

Yet on the other hand, we have those, though few, who have been all quite sure, even eager, to defend the mode of Deleuze's death either as consistent with his own (and Baruch Spinoza's) philosophy, even an apotheosis of it (like Empedocles jumping into the Aetna), or at least as no cause for detraction from his thought. There is, for example, a recent essay by Finn Janning, who, intoning echoes of the *felix culpa* from the Easter *Exsultet,* calls Deleuze's demise a "happy death"![5] To be sure, Janning is not being flippant. He argues that just as "a life worth living" is one with "the power to actualize its own will," so Deleuze committed suicide once having realized that his was no longer that sort of life — i.e., as a way of asserting the *amor fati* (or "being equal to the event") Deleuze had himself acknowledged as the "only ethic" and thus the last actualization of his will.[6] For Janning, Deleuze was living out, embodying his own life affirming philosophy when he jumped out of that lucky window: "I am alive!" would be the translation. It seems fair to say that Janning is reading Deleuze's death in the key of his works and see him as Spinoza's Seneca, a model of inner life "immune" to outside forces (and yet at once driven to death from external force).[7] In all this Janning is no doubt working from the strong monocular desire to see the philosopher and man as one.

In oblique contrast, Didier Éribon had insisted, in an earlier essay titled "Sickness unto Life" published not long after Deleuze's death, that Deleuze's *œuvre* should *not* be reread through the key of his death — implying also the obverse.[8] By way of caution he sites the egregious example of James Miller,

5   Finn Janning, "Happy Death of Deleuze," *Tamara Journal of Critical Organization Inquiry* 11, no. 1 (2013): 29–37.

6   Ibid., 29–31.

7   Spinoza, *Ethics,* IV.A. It is a complex argument Spinoza makes there. Here I am making use of Smith's reading of Deleuze on Spinoza regarding suicide.

8   Didier Éribon, "Sickness unto Life," *Artforum International* 34, no. 7 (March 1996): 35–38.

who through "fabricated quotes," wayward translations, uncriti-
cal, and interpretive "extravagance," sought to sensationalize
Michel Foucault's fateful tango with AIDS as the crowning touch
to his late work,[9] which Deleuze had called *pensée artiste*. Instead, he links the suicide of Deleuze to the descending physical
frailty that presumably triggered it, and points out that it was
that same frailty, which Deleuze had also called "stammering,"
that had served as the very condition of possibility for Deleuzian invention and creativity.[10] For Éribon, there was a thread between the illness and the work, and between the illness and the
death. *C'est tout* — but not the *c'est tout* of a Marguerite Duras,
who thematized her own decline and death in a series of poetic
scribbles leading down to the wispy, if still defiant, end.[11] No, for
Éribon this is a *c'est tout* simpliciter: Deleuze finished his last
book, *Negotiations,* in 1995, and then jumped out. It was a blip
in the "calm grandeur"[12] of a "life of immanence," so to speak.

Finally there is Jason E. Smith's tantalizing essay called "A
Taste for Life (On Some Suicides in Deleuze and Spinoza)." I
say tantalizing because, despite the obvious allusion to and tacit
knowledge of Deleuze's own suicide, Smith keeps quite mum
on it. For that matter, in all his discussion of Deleuze's study
of Foucault and his epithet *pensée artiste* for the latter's late,
"experimental" production, he makes no mention of Foucault's
"knowing" engagement with AIDS either. Instead he buries his
scholarly head in a careful exegesis of how Spinoza and Deleuze
treated suicide. He only tells us (and competently) of the difference between affects and passions in Spinoza and Deleuze,
of how Deleuze conceives the "intensive mode," a mode of im-

9 Ibid., 39.
10 Ibid., 35 and 37, quoting from Gilles Deleuze and Claire Parnet, *Dialogues,*
   trans. Hugh Tomlinson and Barbara Habberjam (New York: Columbia
   University Press, 1987), 5.
11 See her *C'est tout* (1995), translated by Richard Howard as *No More* (New
   York: Seven Stories Press, 1998).
12 I use this Johann Winckelmannian phrase here to mark the stylistic or
   aesthetic choices made even in philosophy — what Deleuze and Guattari
   called *goût* ("taste") in chapter 3 of their last collaboration *What Is Philosophy?*.

munity from external forces, as an auto-affection, etc. He goes as far as to mark his Spinozist-Deleuzian exegesis on suicide by detaching it from Serge Leclaire's formulation, which is in part drawn from the Stoic tradition: "in order to live, I must kill 'myself'; or else I don't really feel alive (this is no life!), therefore I commit suicide."[13] In Smith's reading, Spinoza's neo-Stoic conception never saw suicide as dying "by oneself," because it overestimates the *intensivity* of the will and neglects the extensive forces that perturb and overpower one. For that reason, and he quotes Georges Bernanos in his *Nouvelle histoire de Mouchette,* the suicide's "last glimmer must be one of amazement, of desperate surprise."[14]

Does this surprise, this "frightening suddenness"[15] (again Bernanos), mark every suicide as a surd? Perhaps this is why Smith keeps silent over what he cannot know. Yet it is hard, at some point, not to be drawn into what Maurice Blanchot called the "pure form" of the "second death" — the (impossible) meaning of the event, a noetic postmortem.[16] For one thing, to segregate Deleuze's life from his philosophy of life is not merely to acknowledge his plural selves, but rather to territorialize — against

13  Smith, "A Taste for Life," 83, quoting from Leclaire's book on Robert Bresson's film *Mouchette, A Child is Being Killed,* trans. Marie-Claude Hays (Stanford: Stanford University Press, 1998), 4. Notice the similarity of this syllogism to Janning's reading of Deleuze's "self-donating" death.

14  Smith, "A Taste for Life," 83, quoting from Georges Bernanos, *Nouvelle Histoire de Mouchette* (Paris: Librairie Plon, 1937), 169.

15  Ibid.

16  See for a further discussion of the treatment of this notion, together with that of death, in Blanchot and Deleuze: Harumi Osaki, "Killing Oneself, Killing the Father: On Deleuze's Suicide in Comparison with Blanchot's Notion of Death," *Literature and Theology* 22, no. 1 (2008): 88–101, esp. 89–91. Osaki points out Deleuze's own engagement with Blanchot's ideas on death in his *Logic of Sense,* referenced also by Colombat shortly after Deleuze's death, which Colombat interprets in terms of Blanchot's "second death" (André Pierre Colombat, "November 4, 1995, Deleuze's Death as an Event," *Man and World: An International Philosophical Review* 29 [1996]: 235–49). Cf. also Socrates' account in *The Republic* IV of the man who cannot resist going over to the other side of the road to inspect a dead man lying there, which in that passage is an example of peccable "curiosity" (*polypragmosynē*) (439e 31ff).

his insistence not to — reality.[17] Moreover, his death is there, staring at us, almost as his last challenge to those who would still learn from him: "I won't tell you what this means, but don't ignore it, *mon ami(e)*; think it through for yourself, teach yourself!" After all, jumping out of a window, unlike Seneca or others slitting their veins in a cozy bath or even those hanging themselves, is a very public act. It is a form of self-display, indeed exhibition, even as it also *disfigures* one's countenance and form. You might call it a public self-erasure, a piece of installation art that self-destructs, no less than a suicide bomber.[18]

Still, we should not be content with treating Deleuze's death as just or mainly a matter of biographical interpretation — as "window dressing" on the edifice of a conceptually consistent[19] or exemplary life. Rather we should see in it a further occasion to deterritorialize thought, in homage and continuity to his pluralizing, multiplicative monism, to his singular multiplicity of selves. By multiplicity here I don't mean Deleuze the thinker of life and its affirmation versus Deleuze the morbid or moribund depressive, but rather Deleuze(s) alive and dead. I am interested, taking his idea of becoming animal, in Deleuze the frog, the frog that jumps through earth, air and water, frogs being amphibious between different modes of becoming in life and death. In an auto-affective sense this Deleuze-frog is also its own Hermes Psychopompos, Hermes Conductor-of-Souls who leads them down to Hades — on the way to which, as in Aristophanes' comedy *The Frogs,* one meets many (other) frogs.[20]

Now as Smith points out, death for Spinoza is construed, not as the death of the individual, but rather impersonally, corpore-

17 I say territorialize over and against differentiate or "differenciate" in the Deleuzian sense.

18 Naturally I mean no moral equivalency by this comparison.

19 By "consistent" I mean it not merely in the conventional sense of free of self-contradiction, but in the Deleuzian sense of "*consistant*" as a quality of philosophic concepts that are forged out of elements that stand up and give the concept a solid, autopoetic consistency.

20 See his *Frogs,* where Dionysus and his half-brother Heracles are met by a chorus of frogs on the lake (possibly Acheron, Lake of Woe) on his way to Hades to meet Euripides.

ally; as the change of proportion between motion and rest for a body.[21] This is to be understood as an instantiation of a greater substance, Nature (or God), at work. It is also very much central to and a limit case for his doctrine of affects and passions and hence also Deleuze's own appropriation of it. The distinction between Spinoza's three chief affects, *appetitus* or *cupiditas, laetitia* and *tristitia,* as a matter of the determination of action in higher and lower degrees of perfection (as increased or decreased power to act) is very much relevant to this proportional calculus of motion and rest. If death, including anything we call suicide, is thus conceived, then we may talk about its affective valences, both what leads to it and what it affords affectively.

At the same time, this affective discourse should not be circumscribed within the individual, in this case Deleuze. This is the unfortunate flaw in Janning's analysis of his "happy death." Let's look at it again. He predicates it on Albert Camus' central question of whether life is *worth* living, even as he tries to work Deleuze's defenestration into a Durkheimian context of social integration. He sees Deleuze's life as one of creating and producing concepts, and since Deleuze toward the end of his panting breath could no longer do so, his life had effectively already ended, and was thus not worth living, worth being perhaps a problem in itself. A bit crass maybe? Yet to me this coarse reading is also the point of aperture to the social, the economic and political. Remember the "charm" Deleuze spoke of as consisting of "a sort of awkwardness, a delicacy of health, a frailty of constitution, a vital stammering"?[22] Éribon both regards this as the anchor of invention and creativity, and links it to what Deleuze says in an interview from 1990: "One's always writing to bring something to life, to free life from where it's trapped."[23]

---

21  Spinoza, *Ethics,* II.P13.

22  Éribon, "Sickness unto Life," 35, quoting from Gilles Deleuze and Claire Parnet, *Dialogues,* trans. Hugh Tomlinson and Barbara Habberjam (New York: Columbia University Press, 1987), 5.

23  Ibid., 35, quoting from Gilles Deleuze, *Negotiations: 1972–1990,* trans. Martin Joughin (New York: Columbia University Press, 1995), 141.

As we all know, Deleuze and Félix Guattari published their *Anti-Oedipus* in 1972 not only as a frontal attack on Jacques Lacan, but also as a quixotic lunge at the juggernaut of capitalism and capitalist affects. From then on, Deleuze was always drawing schizoid lines of flight from the regnant political economy and its traps and constructing new assemblages for life. At the same time, his works, his interventions, were always and already part of and reintegrated into the capital he sought to resist. We know, as Deleuze knew, what it is like as scholars and thinkers: People want articles, they want reviews, and if we are good they want interviews, talks, keynote addresses, public debates, and entire books or series. They want us to produce, produce and reproduce, and our existence becomes coefficient with production, which then morphs into a debt that only multiplies itself. The more you produce, the more you owe. But if you don't owe, you're nothing.[24] Deleuze was not innocent of this. He did write, and as a writer could not escape being encased in the structured frame of production.[25] Yet he also studiously avoided debates and interviews, and he hardly traveled or cashed in on lecture circuits or posh American appointments.[26] Janning's analysis

---

24 When I lived in Israel in 2001, I was amazed to hear Israelis voice the following observation: In other countries, people brag about how much they have; the more you have, the richer you are. Here in Israel you hear them *shvits* about how much they owe. The more you owe, the richer you are. Signs of a highly advanced capitalized economy indeed!

25 Cf. stained glass composition of Harm Kamerlingh Onnes in the Algemeen Handelsblad-Gebouw in Amsterdam. This remarkable modernist stained glass composition, commissioned for the hundredth anniversary of the Dutch business newspaper Algemeen Handelsblad in 1927–28 and formerly housed in its building in Amsterdam, shows the newspaper business as a tightly hierarchical network, indeed machine, of specialized roles, from the delivery man to the writer, proofreader and printer to the editor and publisher (counting his money!). The personas are encased not only in twenty leaded frames, but also in a nexus of machinery pertinent to the trade. I evoke this work to illustrate the economic machine into which any writer, Deleuze included, is inserted, much like the Chaplin character in his film *Modern Life.*

26 To be sure, his choices may have been limited by his ill health and the concomitant difficulty of travel.

offers no resistance to this dark side of creativity, and indeed capitulates to the logic of human capital: We live to produce, and by producing can live a "healthy, productive life."[27] The sinister implication is, when we cease to produce, then our lives are over. Publish or perish!

The problem with Janning's reading is that it assumes an exclusionary doctrine of affects and affectivity. Either you have a joyful affect or a sad passion, not both, and either you are increasing your affective potency or letting it slip away — no mixing or blurring please! Spinoza may have sought geometric clarity in triangulating his affects — at least as a heuristic, and in titrating joy and sorrow he was also following the common image in his era of the Laughing and Weeping Philosophers.[28]

This "dyolysis" of affects was also played out in the musical production of his day. From the late 16th century on, music in Europe, perhaps in an attempt to control dissonance in highly chromatic compositions, shifted from the earlier system of the eight church modes to a binary one between the Ionian (major) and the Aeolian (minor) modes. In the theory and practice of the 17th into the 18th century, precisely when capitalism also underwent its definitive launch through the Dutch and the English and their global exploits, the major mode came to be associated with happy affects and the minor with the sad, both under the regime of pre-established harmony (Leibniz). In this harmonic regime an amalgamation of the major and minor was strictly forbidden; only one main affect was allowed in each movement

27 This is precisely what the Bill and Melinda Gates Foundation claims as its goal for everyone in the world. See http://www.gatesfoundation.org.

28 A representative image here is the *Democritus and Heraclitus* by Cornelis Stangerus, 1662. This motif of the Weeping Heraclitus and the Laughing Democritus was quite popular in 17th-century Netherlands, the chief node of early global capitalism of the time, but had been established by Donato Bramante in 1477, following the ancient epithets for the two philosophers. The laughter of Democritus had been construed as the scoffing laughter of a disillusioned thinker, but in 17th-century art it seems to have been interpreted more "naively" — closer to how Spinoza conceived of happy (versus sad) affects.

or piece.[29] This polarity of tonal affect largely persisted in more learned musical *Tonkunst* until the end of tonality a century ago, though it has lingered in various other ways up through our day, in popular as well as high art genres.[30] Franz Schubert was, however, a rebel against this dichotomy in the 19th century, and constantly tried to subvert it by erasing the solidity of either tonal affect (e.g., Allegretto in C-minor, D. 915),[31] while a century later Arnold Schönberg and his pupils would demolish it with their atonality,[32] even as Béla Bartók, Charles Ives, Igor Stravinsky, and Darius Milhaud all vexed it with their experiments in bitonality.[33]

Deleuze may have done something similar when he reconceived Spinoza's happy affects as *passive* affects (hence passions) along with the sad, and reserved the active affect only for what he called auto-affection, the affect immune from extensive force. Bill Clinton, in eulogizing the African-American historian John

29  This same doctrine of affects applied to the development of the modern prose composition by single-thesis paragraphs.

30  This binary affectivity is also strongly reflected in the like/dislike dispositive of internet culture, and in the dichotomous symbols for "happy" and "sad" :-) and :-( or :) and :( and their various emoji cognates used in emails and instant messaging today.

31  In fact, Schubert's subversion of the tonal tradition went as far as to invert the conventional affects associated with the major and minor modes, at times making the major sound sad and wistful and the minor jolly — even jaunty. Evidence of this could be observed in the Andante of his Symphony No. 9 and Moment Musical No. 3. In this sense he was not only a master of tonality (as in full display in his String Quintet in C), but also its great ironist.

32  This first occurred in Schönberg's free atonal works from 1908 to 1923, and then with his twelve-tone technique from 1921 on (preceded by an early experiment in the Third of Bartók's *Fourteen Bagatelles* of 1908), with refinements by his pupil Anton Webern.

33  For early examples of the simultaneous bitonality in early Modernist composition, which roughly coincided with free atonality and the early development of dodecaphony in the Second Viennese School led by Schönberg, cf. Bartók's *Fourteen Bagatelles* (1908, the third of which also adumbrated dodecaphony), Ives's *Variations on America* (1909–10), Stravinsky's *Rite of Spring* (1913), and Milhaud's *Petites Symphonies* (1917–22). In such works, the superposition of one key over another effectively disrupts the conventional affective associations of tonal harmony.

Hope Franklin (1915–2009), called him the "happiest angry man I know, and the angriest happy man I know."[34] Yet in being a co-affective man and a forceful historian of resistance, Franklin was also rising above the passive affects.

Deleuze would have appreciated this. He thought of auto-affection as "folding" or "straddling."[35] For him it was a strategy not of reaction but of refusal and neutralization, much as in judo. He wrote to "free life from where it's trapped,"[36] and may have died also to escape the trap of capitalist production as a production of capitalist affects — either happy or sad, either producing more or producing less — on the upswing or depressed, just like its market and its meds.[37] Deleuze's defenestration may be seen here not merely as an escape from the judgment of capital on an unproductive cripple, but as an unframing of its binary affective framework. It allows philosophy and philosophers, like the two great philosophers of change in Antiquity, to cry and to laugh — even at once, but in such passional *Durcharbeit* arrive at an auto-affection that is still pathopoetic (cf. the gagaku work Etenraku 越天樂, or *Transcelestial Joy*).[38] As Plato's Eleatic Stranger says in *The Sophist*: "being (*einai*) is the power (*dynamis*) to act (*poiein*) and undergo (*paschein*)."[39] In other words it affects and is affected. The only word we need there to clarify the matter is *hama*, at once, which is also the temporality of auto-affect. Only then can we see Deleuze's *terror* of meeting striped *terra firma* deterritorialize and liquefy again.

---

34  Bill Clinton, at memorial service in Duke University Chapel, June 11, 2009 (author's recollection). A press report of the time simply related the expression as "[a]n angry, happy man. A happy, angry man," (http://www.blueridgenow.com/article/20090612/NEWS/906129983).

35  Smith, "A Taste for Life," 76, referring to Deleuze, *Negotiations*, 98.

36  Éribon, "Sickness unto Life," 35, quoting from Deleuze, *Negotiations*, 141.

37  This chain of binaries is in turn a motive component in the modern ideology of progress, invented in the 17th century.

38  This is a classical Japanese piece descended from the Chinese court repertoire forged in the unlikely crucible of shamanistic music from the early Silk Road mixed with Confucian aesthetics of noble "apathy."

39  Plato, *The Sophist*, 247d–e; translation mine.

# Biographies

**Samantha Bankston** is an Associate Professor of Philosophy at Sierra Nevada College in the United States. In 2013 she translated Anne Sauvagnargues' book, *Deleuze and Art,* for Bloomsbury/ Continuum into English. In 2014 she was invited to the University of Copenhagen as a visiting scholar to work on her first authored book, *Deleuze and Becoming(s)* (Bloomsbury Publishing). Her book *Deleuze and Žizek* will be published by Palgrave Macmillan, and she has published articles on and translations of Deleuze, Foucault, and Beauvoir in a variety of edited volumes. She is part of an international team that transcribes Deleuze's unpublished, audio-recorded lectures from the University of Paris-8 at http://www.webdeleuze.com.

**Benoît Dillet** holds a PhD from the University of Kent and works as a Junior Research Fellow at the Freiburg Institute for Advanced Studies (FRIAS), University of Freiburg, Germany. He is the co-editor of *The Edinburgh Companion to Poststructuralism* (Edinburgh University Press, 2013) and *Technologiques: La Pharmacie de Bernard Stiegler* (Cécile Defaut, 2013).

**Moritz Gansen** is currently a doctoral candidate in philosophy at Technische Universität Darmstadt, where he investigates the receptions and transformations of Anglo-American pragmatism and empiricism in French twentieth-century philosophy. Other research interests include aesthetics and politics, the entangled histories of recent European philosophy, and methods and perspectives for writing and teaching the history of philosophy. Besides these academic pursuits, he works as an editor and translator.

**Arjen Kleinherenbrink** is a Doctoral Candidate in Philosophy and coordinator of the Center for Contemporary European Philosophy at the Radboud University Nijmegen in the Netherlands. His current research focuses on Deleuze's ontology, a project nested within a more general pursuit of the implications of twentieth and twenty-first century philosophy for contemporary organization theory. He is the translator of Deleuze's *What is Grounding?,* and has published articles on themes including authenticity, territoriality, and freedom in thinkers such as Bergson, Kant, Kierkegaard, and Deleuze and Guattari.

**David Liu** is a Visiting Scholar (formerly visiting faculty) at Duke University. He has taught and presented widely in religion, language and literature, theory and philosophy, traversing various cultural-temporal divides. He likes giving transdisciplinary and -historical courses on pressing contemporary issues, or those on specific works in the original (lately Boethius, Deleuze, Weil). His main projects are to construct a transcultural, post-Deleuzian metaphysics and a theory of posthumanist culture called "curiosity." Recent writings include comparative essays on "religion" in East Asia and on Daoist (me)ontology. In his imaginary spare time David also translates philosophic (and) poetic texts and researches his native Taiwanese as a literary language in Han characters.

**Ceciel Meiborg** holds a BA in Philosophy from Erasmus University Rotterdam and an MA in Modern European Philosophy from Kingston University, London, where she graduated with a master's dissertation on Whitehead's process philosophy. She has co-written an article which proposes a speculative, Deleuzian differentiation of mannerism and baroque in music and music theory, which has been published in *Diacritics* (2014). She has received a Fulbright scholarship for the continuation of her studies in Philosophy at the New School for Social Research in

New York. Her research interests include philosophy of music, aesthetics, political philosophy, process philosophy and speculative philosophy.

**Jason Read** is Associate Professor of Philosophy at the University of Southern Maine. He teaches courses in the history of political philosophy, contemporary social theory, the politics of work, philosophy of film, and philosophy of history. He is the author of *The Micro-Politics of Capital: Marx and the Prehistory of the Present* (SUNY Press, 2003) and *The Politics of Transindividuality* (Brill/Haymarket, 2015), as well as articles on Althusser, Deleuze, Spinoza, Hegel, Negri, and *The Wire*.

**Louis-Georges Schwartz** is a scholar and activist who heads the MA Program in Film Studies at Ohio University. He is the author of a short book on the case law controlling the use of film and video evidence in United States Courts entitled *Mechanical Witness*. He has also written articles on free indirect style in cinema, Bazinian photographic ontology, the genealogy of the concept "life." On the latter subject he edited a special issue of *Discourse*. He is currently working on a project seeking to introduce historical materialist methodology to Film Studies by positing a third Deleuzian image type. As an activist Schwartz works with organizations seeking to establish dual power in North America, in part through screenings of *La Commune, 1871* at free schools. Schwartz opposes the racist oppression faced by Atlanta's proletariate and supports University divestment and cultural boycott of the Zionist apartheid state.

**Sjoerd van Tuinen** is Assistant Professor in Philosophy at Erasmus University Rotterdam and coordinator of the Centre for Art and Philosophy. In 2009 he received his PhD for a dissertation on Deleuze and Leibniz, entitled *Mannerism in Philosophy,* at Ghent University. He is editor of numerous books, including *Deleuze and The Fold: A Critical Reader* (Palgrave Macmillan, 2010), *Deleuze compendium* (Boom, 2009), *De nieuwe Franse filosofie* (Boom, 2011), *Giving and Taking: Antidotes to a Culture* *of Greed* (V2/NAi, 2014), and has authored *Sloterdijk: Binnenste-buiten denken* (Klement, 2004). Van Tuinen has been awarded a VENI scholarship from the Netherlands Organisation for Scientific Research (2012–16) for a research project on ressentiment and democracy. He is currently finalizing a monograph in which he proposes a philosophical concept of mannerism, entitled *Matter, Manner, Idea: Deleuze and Mannerism.*